RACINE

Bérénice

James J. Supple

Lecturer in French,
University of St Andrews

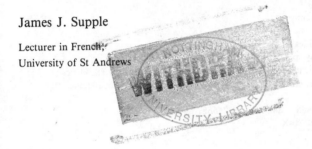

NOTTINGHAM
WITHDRAWN
UNIVERSITY LIBRARY

Grant & Cutler Ltd
1986

© Grant & Cutler Ltd
1986

314119

Library of Congress Cataloging-in-Publication Data

Supple, James J.
   Racine, Bérénice.

   (Critical guides to French texts: 57)
   Bibliography: p.
   1. Racine, Jean, 1639-1699. Bérénice. 2. Berenice, b. ca. 28, in fiction, drama, poetry, etc. 3. Bible in literature. I. Title. II. Title: Bérénice. III. Series.
PQ1893.S8 1986   842'.4   86-25668
ISBN 0-7293-0230-X

I.S.B.N. 84-599-1741-X

DEPÓSITO LEGAL: V. 2.253 - 1986

Printed in Spain by
Artes Gráficas Soler, S.A., Valencia
for
GRANT & CUTLER LTD
55-57, GREAT MARLBOROUGH STREET, LONDON W1V 2AY
and
27, SOUTH MAIN STREET, WOLFEBORO, NH 03894-2069, USA

6 00 314119 9

TELEPEN

Critical Guides to French Texts

57 Racine. Bérénice

Critical Guides to French Texts

EDITED BY ROGER LITTLE, WOLFGANG VAN EMDEN, DAVID WILLIAMS

For my Racine students
past and present, at the
University of St Andrews.

Contents

Contents

Prefatory Note

Bérénice could be studied from a variety of angles but two appear to be especially important, particularly for undergraduates. First, how does *Bérénice* work as a play? Second, how does it work as a tragedy? My experience of teaching Racine inclines me to think that the first of these problems is the one which causes students most difficulty. I have, in consequence, accorded it most of my attention here. Chapters 1-4 attempt to show how the play is structured and to analyse the dramatic effects which it produces. Chapter 5 is devoted to an examination of the tragic implications of the play. My ultimate intention, however, is to show how the dramatic and tragic patterns created by Racine coalesce in the final scene when Bérénice regains her tragic stature at the same time as she provides the play with its unexpected ending.

All line references are to the Nouveaux Classiques Larousse edition by L. Lejealle of 1971. Italicized numbers in parentheses followed by page references refer to the corresponding items in the bibliography at the end of this volume.

It is a pleasure to acknowledge the assistance kindly given by David Williams and Wolfgang van Emden (advisory editiors), also by Ian Higgins, Tony Hunt and Jill Munro, all of whom read my typescript and made many valuable suggestions.

1. 'Faire quelque chose de rien'

'Titus, qui aimait passionément Bérénice, et qui même, à ce qu'on croyait, lui avait promis de l'épouser, la renvoya de Rome, malgré lui et malgré elle, dès les premiers jours de son empire.' Racine's subject as summarized in his preface (p.27) seems to exemplify one of the most important problems faced by the English-speaking student encountering seventeenth-century French tragedy for the first time: the apparent lack of dramatic action. Although closely related to the more eventful tragicomedy from which it had in large measure sprung, seventeenth-century French tragedy offers a marked contrast with Elizabethan and Jacobean drama. Whereas Shakespeare portrays the duel between Hamlet and Laertes as well as 'alarums' on the field of battle, Corneille (whose plays contain considerably more external events than Racine's) has Rodrigue in *Le Cid* fight both Don Gomès and the invading Moors offstage.

Many reasons have been advanced for this, ranging from a Counter-Reformation desire to banish unseemly action from the stage to an inadequate understanding of the extent to which the audience is prepared to suspend its disbelief; but they need not detain us here. It is more important to note for our purposes that *Bérénice*, though often referred to as the most typical example of Racine's art (see *41*), is really a *cas-limite*. It is, indeed, a deliberate attempt on Racine's part to simplify his plot in a way which is far more radical than anything he attempted either before or after. *Andromaque*, his first great success (1667), is based on a love-triangle worthy of a pastoral novel (Hermione loves Pyrrhus, who loves Andromaque). It is further complicated by the fact that Andromaque is still in love with her dead husband, while Hermione is pursued by Oreste. It is from this complicated network of relationships that the catastrophic dénouement of the play will spring: Pyrrhus is assassinated;

Oreste, still spurned by Hermione, goes mad; and Hermione herself commits suicide. In *Britannicus*, the play which preceded *Bérénice* by one year (1669), the love plot is simpler (Britannicus's love for Junie is reciprocated); but the situation is complicated by the fact that Nero is infatuated with Junie, and determined to make an issue of his mother's apparent support for Britannicus, whom he poisons in order to establish his political and psychological independence. In *Bajazet*, which was first performed in 1672 (two years after *Bérénice*), we find a similar pattern. Roxane, jealous of Atalide, whose love is returned by Bajazet, sends the unattainable object of her love to his death, just before being struck down herself by the sultan, whom she has betrayed. Atalide then commits suicide on stage. Compared with plots like these, *Bérénice* seems to offer little scope for dramatic exploitation.

The reason which Racine gives for his choice of topic (preface, pp.27-28) is that he wished to emulate the 'simplicité d'action qui a été si fort du goût des anciens'. The models which he mentions are all plays by Sophocles, whose work certainly fascinated him. It is not difficult, however, to detect behind Racine's words an attack on Corneille, whose status as the leading exponent of French tragedy he was determined to win for himself. It was, indeed, Corneille who, more than anybody, was responsible for transforming early seventeenth-century tragi-comedy into the genre which we now call 'classical tragedy'. In *Horace*, in particular, he focused his attention on a crisis situation and manipulated the plot in a way which highlighted the emotional, moral and psychological dilemmas of the protagonists. In doing so, he found it easy for the first time to obey the unities of time and place, which academic critics like the Abbé d'Aubignac were trying to impose. In many of his subsequent plays, however, he returned to the much more involved plots which his younger rival derided as fundamentally implausible. The change of policy on Corneille's part was deliberate and derived directly from his very different view of the emotions which drama should seek to create;[1] but it also

_____

[1] Notably wonder and amazement — hence his affirmation in the "Au Lecteur" to *Héraclius*: 'le sujet d'une belle tragédie doit n'être pas vraisemblable'. See

provided Racine with a golden opportunity to elevate simplicity of plot into an aesthetic principle which would allow him once and for all to establish his superiority (*9*, p.134). Whereas Corneille claimed that complicated plays present the dramatist with a real test of his skill (see the *Examen de Cinna*), Racine adopted a diametrically opposed position:

> Il y en a qui pensent que cette simplicité est une marque de peu d'invention. Ils ne songent pas qu'au contraire toute l'invention consiste à faire quelque chose de rien, et que tout ce grand nombre d'incidents a toujours été le refuge des poètes [i.e. dramatists] qui ne sentaient pas dans leur génie ni assez d'abondance ni assez de force pour attacher durant cinq actes leurs spectateurs par une action simple, soutenue de la violence des passions, de la beauté des sentiments et de l'élégance de l'expression. (Preface, p.28)

This barbed challenge to Corneille was not made solely on the theoretical plane. It is difficult for us to know now whether both dramatists were persuaded to attempt the same subject by Henriette d'Angleterre, or if one of them deliberately pirated the other's subject (see *3*, *40*, *41*, *45*). My own impression is that Corneille probably copied Racine. It is clear, however, that their long-standing rivalry came to a head when they both produced plays on the separation of Titus and Bérénice within days of each other.

Aware that his younger rival was challenging him on the issues of simplicity and *vraisemblance* (a similar attack had featured in the first preface to *Britannicus*), Corneille produced a play which is much simpler than most of his later work. Crucially, however, he felt the need to complicate the plot by basing it on two pairs of lovers. Tite loves Bérénice, and is loved by her; but, knowing that the Romans will disapprove of a match with a foreign queen, he has resolved to marry Domitie, a dynastically well-placed Roman noblewoman. The latter loves Tite's brother, Domitien, but prefers a union with the emperor, which would

H.T. Barnwell (editor), *Pierre Corneille: writings on the theatre* (Oxford: Blackwell, 1965), p.190.

gratify her ambition. Domitien, who loves her, is none too
pleased with this, and is delighted when his *confident* arranges
for Bérénice's surprise return to the imperial court in the
justified hope that her physical proximity will weaken Tite's
resolve. This creates multiple possibilities. Will the emperor
marry Bérénice? and, if so, will Domitie marry Domitien and
support a rebellion against Tite? If he does not marry Bérénice,
will he go ahead with his plans to marry Domitie and/or let his
brother marry the foreign queen? Alternatively, will he abdicate,
thus allowing Domitie to marry the new occupant of the throne?
In the event, a different solution is found: Tite decides that, if he
cannot marry the woman he loves, he will not marry anyone.
This leaves the way open for Domitie to marry Domitien, who
becomes heir apparent.

Racine, for his part, is equally unable to construct a five-act
play with only two major characters; but he contents himself
with the invention of Antiochus, who is not only the friend of
both Titus and Bérénice but also the queen's former suitor. He
hopes to win her hand if she is rejected by the emperor, but is, as
he rightly realizes (l.49), 'un amant sans espoir'. His main
dramatic function is fourfold but none the less limited. By
revealing his secret love for Bérénice to his *confident* in Act I, he
provides the audience with the information which they need
about himself, Titus and Bérénice if they are to understand the
way in which the plot will unfold. He acts as a messenger
between Titus and Bérénice in Act III. He helps increase the
pressures on Titus at the end of Act IV when he pleads with him
to return to the queen. Finally, the spectacle of his suffering and
the example of his self-abnegation help to motivate Bérénice's
decision to sacrifice her own happiness in the final scene of the
play. We will see later that he also has a role as a moral exemplar
against which the initially weak and often selfish behaviour of
the main protagonists can be judged. One can understand,
however, why so many critics have doubted whether Antiochus
really has an integral role to play in *Bérénice* (e.g. Venesoen, *30*,
p.289, n.10).

The problems which Racine set himself by writing a play with
such a limited number of main characters and with such a

limited subject are well defined in the first preface to
Britannicus, where he describes his ideal subject as 'simple,
chargé de peu de matière', as 's'avançant par degrés vers sa fin',
and as being sustained only by 'les intérêts, les sentiments et les
passions des personnages'. I will try to analyse the techniques he
uses in order to overcome these problems in the next three
chapters. I would like for the moment to focus on two of the
ways in which he exploits a convention which students who are
new to seventeenth-century French tragedy might be tempted to
regard as unduly restricting: the unity of place.

Far from exacerbating his problems, Racine's decision to limit
the scene to 'un cabinet [...] entre l'appartement de Titus et celui
de Bérénice' permits him to give symbolic expression to the
emperor's fate. Desiring a private meeting with Bérénice,
Antiochus explains to Arsace at the beginning of the play that he
has chosen the antechamber which the emperor himself uses
when he wishes to be alone. Titus's need for privacy before his
father's death was not, however, the result of a simple desire to
escape from the attentions of the courtiers. Vespasian, like 'le
peuple, le sénat, tout l'empire romain' (l.1077), disapproved of
his liaison with a foreign queen and tried to end it. It was only in
secret, therefore, that Titus could give full expression to his love.
Now, however, the 'cabinet superbe et solitaire' (l.3) has been
opened up to the gaze of the outside world, symbolized by
Antiochus, Arsace, Paulin, Rutile and, of course, the spectator.
As a result of this, the emperor's private life will inevitably have
to be subordinated to his public duties. The *cabinet*, which has
witnessed the depth of his passion for Bérénice and which is still
festooned with their intertwined initials (ll.1324-25), is about to
become the scene for their bitter quarrel in Act IV scene 5, and,
subsequently, for their heart-rending separation. The queen
avails herself of this fact, naturally enough, to intensify her
reproaches when accusing Titus of betraying her love for him
(ll.1109, 1320-26).

The symbolic value of the *cabinet* is exploited even more
brilliantly at the end of Act IV. Having been told by Titus that
he wants her to go, the queen rushes off into her apartment
threatening suicide. Her anguish is so great that Antiochus

pleads with the emperor to follow her. At the same time, Rutile enters with the news that the representatives of the Roman people are asking for an audience. In this way, Titus's conflicting passions are externalized on the stage. His heart tells him to follow Bérénice; but his sense of duty, reinforced by the interventions of both Rutile and Paulin, inclines him to answer the summons from the senators. He is caught, like Hercules at the crossroads, between two different paths: the path to duty symbolized by the door to his apartment; and the path leading to personal happiness, represented by the door to Bérénice's rooms. Racine's apparently limited set provides in this way spatial expression to the emperor's dilemma.

Adherence to the unity of place also makes it possible for Racine to create the uncertainties without which he would find it impossible to develop his limited material to the full. Once we have seen or read the play, we know that Titus's decision to increase the size of Bérénice's kingdom is no more than a despairing attempt to soften the blow of their separation (ll.528-30, 759-66). Bérénice, however, assumes, wrongly but understandably, that the gifts which he is having confirmed by the senate are proof of his intention to marry her (ll.169-77). She also misconstrues his later visit to the senate, which takes place between the end of Act IV and the beginning of Act V. Now convinced that he is cruelly and gratuitously rejecting her, she believes that he has gone to be congratulated for complying with the Romans' wishes (ll.1328-34). Titus, in fact, had gone to the senate only because he felt that he could not disobey its summons and had remained unmoved by its plaudits (ll.1245-46, 1375-79). On each occasion, the queen's error can only serve to make her predicament worse. This both complicates and extends the plot, as does Arsace's erroneous interpretation of the queen's own decision to leave Rome at the beginning of Act V. This is no more than a ploy to which she resorts in order to escape from the surveillance of those whom Titus has instructed to prevent her from committing suicide (ll.1201-04): once outside Rome, she intends to go ahead with her plan (ll.1359-61). Both Antiochus and Titus are taken in by her manœuvre, however. The former is led to give tentative expression to his hopes of winning her on the rebound (ll.1279-84), while the latter is so deceived that the discovery of her real intentions galvanizes him into making the ultimatum (agree to remain alive or *I* will commit suicide) which will eventually provide the play with its dénouement (ll.1363 ff.).

This sense of uncertainty is extended, at various points in the play, to include the influence of Rome. The Romans' views on Bérénice are certain enough. Although otherwise totally subservient to their emperors, they still remember the Tarquins (the early Roman monarchs who were banished following the rape of Lucretia), and conserve an undying hatred for the whole concept of kingship. As Bérénice is a queen and, of necessity, a foreign queen, she is regarded as a doubly impossible match for Titus (ll.376-419). The emperor is aware of this from the outset (ll.446-50) and, in general, very anxious to live up to Rome's expectations (ll.467-70, 1155-74). There are two moments in the play, however, when he is so distressed by Bérénice's suffering that he is tempted to reject the Roman viewpoint (ll.1216, 1319). More insidiously still, he allows himself in a moment of vain but understandable wishful-thinking to try to convince himself that the love and virtues displayed by Bérénice are so great that Rome might actually be persuaded to approve of their marriage (see below p.45).

This attempt at self-deception is too obvious for Titus to delude himself for long; but the emperor also suffers from another problem. With his new-found desire to do his duty, he finds it necessary to send Bérénice away *before* he is actually obliged to do so. He is, in part, motivated by a sympathetic desire to spare Bérénice the humiliation which she might experience at the hands of a Roman mob (ll.732-34), but he is also keen to act early enough to make sure that he and the queen may gain some credit from making a voluntary decision to separate: 'Sauvons de cet affront mon nom et sa mémoire;/Et, puisqu'il faut céder, cédons à notre gloire' (ll.735-36). This makes it harder for Bérénice to understand the necessity for what is happening to her. This is why she reproaches him for sending her away before the Romans have demanded that she should go ('Lorsque Rome se tait', l.1084), and asks him despairingly why she cannot remain in Rome if she agrees not to marry him: 'Hé bien, Seigneur, hé bien, qu'en peut-il arriver?/Voyez-vous les Romains prêts à s'élever?' (ll.1137-38).

One critic has utilized this argument to support his suggestion that Titus no longer loves Bérénice and is just using Rome's traditional hatred of everything to do with monarchy as a convenient excuse to send her away (see *10*, pp.97-98). To argue in this way is, however, to deny the evidence of the text. Titus *does* love Bérénice (see below pp.72-73) and he is also very conscious of the pressure which Rome is exerting on him. As emperor, he will, in the end, have to make a personal decision; but that decision will be made in the light of the constraints which are placed upon him. He is aware, as we will see in the final chapter, that these constraints lack any logical basis; but he feels none the less that he cannot escape from them:

> Ma gloire inexorable à toute heure me suit;
> Sans cesse elle présente à mon âme étonnée
> L'empire incompatible avec votre hyménée.
>
>   (1394-96)

The unruly Roman mob is obviously excluded from the emperor's secret antechamber, but it can still make its influence felt on Titus, who is constantly aware of watching eyes: 'Rome observe aujourd'hui ma conduite nouvelle', as he tells Paulin in Act II ll.(467, cf. ll.339-44). The strength of Roman opposition to his liaison with Bérénice has been forcibly impressed on him in the past (ll.1019-22), and Paulin delightedly informs him during the course of the play of Rome's enthusiastic reception of the rumour that she is to be sent away (ll.1220-24). Bérénice herself reacts bitterly to the sound of Roman joy when her plans to flee from Rome become known in Act V (ll.1312-16). In this way, Rome actually becomes a character whose influence is all the harder to escape because it is an unseen presence which both exerts pressures on the protagonists and reacts to their decisions.

2. Dramatic Structure

One of the other main seventeenth-century dramatic conventions (the unity of time, which decreed that the events in a play should all take place within twenty-four hours at the outside) sometimes created difficulties for Corneille, who often needed to compress numerous events in a manner which accentuated rather than reduced their fundamental *invraisemblance*. Racine's task in *Bérénice* is the different but no less difficult problem of expanding a slim plot in such a way that it can realistically occupy five acts. His preface makes it clear that he felt that he had succeeded. He makes a jibe at Corneille ('quelle vraisemblance y a-t-il qu'il arrive en un jour une multitude de choses qui pourraient à peine arriver en plusieurs semaines?'), and clearly boasts of his own ability to 'attacher [ses] spectateurs par une action simple, soutenue de la violence des passions, de la beauté des sentiments et de l'élégance de l'expression' (p.28).

Discussion of the two latter elements may be postponed for the time being; but the relationship between 'une action simple' and 'la violence des passions' requires comment. The main reason why Racine finds it easy in all his tragedies to comply with the unity of time is that his plots centre not so much on events as on the characters' emotions and psychology. It should be noted, none the less, that the relationship between plot and passion is a reciprocal relationship. The plot is based on the evolving emotions and reactions of the characters; but these emotions and reactions are themselves manipulated, and continually exacerbated, by the plot itself. It is this interplay between plot and passion which enables Racine to develop his chosen situation in such a way that it will advance 'par degrés vers sa fin' and, in doing so, grip the spectator during five acts (see above p.13). *Bérénice* does not build up to the almost melodramatic climaxes of *Mithridate* and *Bajazet*; but it is, in its own way, just as dramatic. It is certainly *not* the simple elegiac lament that Sainte-Beuve claimed it to be (quoted in *4*, p.118).

Proving the veracity of this assertion will require detailed analysis of the structure of the play as a whole. Before we embark on this, we should note that, despite its apparent simplicity, Racine's plot is in fact double. The title of the play tends to suggest that Bérénice is the principal protagonist. She is certainly the (at first) uncomprehending victim of Titus's decision to send her away. It is natural, therefore, that our main concern should be to see how she will react to her fate. It is self-evident, however, that Bérénice can make up her own mind about what she is to do only when Titus has finally managed to make his own decision. In a sense, he has already done so before the play commences. Thus, in Act II scene 2, he invites Paulin to inform him of what the Roman people really feel about Bérénice, and then explains: 'Si je t'ai fait parler, si j'ai voulu t'entendre,/Je voulais que ton zèle achevât en secret/De confondre un amour qui se tait à regret' (ll.448-50). Titus had hoped, before his father's death, to marry Bérénice when he became emperor. This was theoretically possible because the corrupt Roman people had long since learned to pander to its ruler's whims (ll.349-54); but Titus's newly developed sense of duty overwhelmed him once he found himself in the wished-for position (ll.459-62). He feels obliged, therefore, to dismiss Bérénice. The problem, however, is that, though he is prepared to ignore the suffering which the separation will cause him (ll.551-52), he cannot bear to inflict pain on a woman he loves so dearly (ll.993-99). It is as a result of this (very sympathetic) weakness that he finds himself unable to acquaint Bérénice with her fate in Act II scene 4, and actually wavers in Act IV scene 5 and in Act V scene 5, when he tells her that she may stay (ll.1130, 1312).

It is misleading to suggest, therefore, that Bérénice controls the plot (*2*, p.xxxii; *41*, p.200). It *is* Bérénice's change of heart which resolves matters in the closing lines of the play; but she is unable to make a decisive move until Titus has convinced her of the inevitability of his decision and of the genuineness of his motives. This he does not successfully do until the later part of Act V scene 6. It is important to realize this for two reasons.

First, because it casts light on the way in which Racine builds his play up to a dramatic (and unexpected) climax. Second, because it shows us how the playwright expands his material. By endowing Titus with a fundamental inability to see Bérénice suffer, he makes him waver; and this wavering actually makes Bérénice's suffering worse. As a result of this, she is over-whelmed with feelings of bewilderment and betrayal which cause her to lash out and to hurt Titus in return. His feelings of pain are thereby increased and his resolve weakened still further — so much so that, when he comes to see her at the beginning of Act V, he no longer knows exactly what he is going to do (l.1382). His suicide threat, which is as much the product of his despair as it is of any rational resolve (see below, pp.80, 82), finally con-vinces the queen that, though there will be no reprieve for her, she is loved by Titus. Secure in this knowledge, she can finally find the strength to go, thus providing the play with its bloodless conclusion. It should not be forgotten, however, that the suicide threat which pulls the scales from Bérénice's eyes at the moment when Titus expects it least (moral blackmail has replaced his earlier efforts at persuasion) is the culmination of all of the emperor's sufferings hitherto. The bulk of the play is based on the spectacle of two people who love each other desperately, but who are driven, as a result of the terrible situation in which they unexpectedly find themselves, to cause each other more and more pain. It is this *machine infernale* which creates the 'violence des passions' of which Racine boasts in his preface.

Before beginning a more detailed study of Racine's plot, it will be as well to point out to students new to seventeenth-century drama that no plot ever follows a pre-ordained plan (see 9, chapter 4). It is because it does not that different dramatists can write different plays on the same subject: Corneille and Racine on the separation of Titus and Bérénice, or Racine and Pradon on Phaedra's incestuous love for Hippolytus, for example. From our point of view, it is essential to remember that the disposition of Racine's plot is the result of conscious strategies adopted to exploit his limited material in such a way that it can create the maximum dramatic, emotional and psychological impact. The best way to understand these

strategies is to approach the plot from Racine's point of view as
a practising dramatist and to ask oneself a number of the
questions which he almost certainly asked himself. Which
characters should be on stage at what time? Who should be on
stage with whom? What advantages can be achieved by
juxtaposing different scenes? And what effects can be created by
granting the audience more knowledge than that vouchsafed to
the various protagonists? The answers to these questions will
help us to see how Racine creates and manipulates dramatic
tension, how he makes us conscious of terrible dramatic ironies,
and how he brings the emotional and psychological development
of his characters to a climax in the final scene.

The beginning of Act I is given over to Antiochus for two
reasons. First, he is the most passive of the three major
characters: it is important, therefore, to enlist our sympathies
for him at an early stage. Second, as he has loved Bérénice in
secret for five years, and is only now revealing that love to his
confident, he is in an excellent position to acquaint the audience
with the realities of the situation as he sees them whilst
ostensibly informing Arsace. One could argue that it is rather
improbable that he would have kept his passion secret from his
confident; but this minor blemish is dwarfed by the dramatic
contrast created by introducing Antiochus and allowing him to
give expression to his forlorn love for Bérénice before bringing
the queen herself onto the stage. Where Antiochus is sad and
tremulous (l.21), the queen is only too happy to escape from the
self-seeking courtiers who have been besieging her in the belief
that she is about to become empress (ll.135-38). She has been
somewhat alarmed by Titus's strange behaviour during the past
week (ll.151-58), but joyfully assumes that the emperor is indeed
about to marry her (ll.164-77). In so doing, she unintentionally
wounds the hapless Antiochus, whose declaration of love five
years earlier she has apparently forgotten (ll.189-204). Knowing
that he still loves her, we can appreciate the dramatic irony. His
declared intention of revealing his love also fills us with anguish
since Bérénice's evident infatuation with Titus enables us to
guess how his confession will be received: with shock and anger
(ll.209, 259-64). Ironically, however, it is her attempt to soften

the blow by expressing regret at the imminent departure of a man who has been such a friend to Titus as well as to her ('Titus vous chérissait, vous admiriez Titus./Cent fois je me suis fait une douceur extrême/D'entretenir Titus dans un autre lui-même') which exacerbates his sufferings. It reminds him that he has only ever been second-best: 'Et c'est ce que je fuis. J'évite, mais trop tard,/Ces cruels entretiens où je n'ai point de part' (ll.273-74).

Having been wounded in this way, Antiochus naturally leaves the stage to Bérénice and her *confidente*. This gives Racine the opportunity he requires to acquaint us with the queen's hopes and emotions before he introduces Titus at the beginning of the next act. Her total devotion to Titus has been obvious enough during her conversation with Antiochus, but it becomes more evident still as she evokes with rapturous enthusiasm the ceremonies of the previous night. In her mind, these ceremonies were devoted not so much to the deification of the dead Vespasian (their true function) as to the apotheosis of the new emperor, around whom her world revolves:

> Ciel! avec quel respect et quelle complaisance
> Tous les cœurs en secret l'assuraient de leur foi!
> Parle: peut-on le voir sans penser, comme moi,
> Qu'en quelque obscurité que le ciel l'eût fait naître
> Le monde en le voyant eût reconnu son maître?
>
> (312-16)

We see here a perfect example of the way in which Racine can *exploit* the unities of time and place. As the ceremony was held the previous day and in another place, it cannot figure directly in his play. By having it described by Bérénice, on the other hand, Racine can achieve two positive effects. He can make it clear that her love for Titus is such that she *wants* him to be emperor — which is crucial, as we shall see (below, pp.83-84), for the dénouement of the play. Also, he can re-create the emotional pattern with which one is familiar from so many seventeenth-century tragedies, most of which move from expected happiness to ultimate disaster. It is noteworthy, indeed, that the very intensity of Bérénice's re-creation of the previous evening's proceedings leads us to suspect that she is unwise to give herself over to her joy so unreservedly. She seems half aware of this herself ('Mais, Phénice, où m'emporte un souvenir charmant?', l.317), but her obsession with Titus is too strong to allow reality to break in. It is often the function of *confidents* and *confidentes*, on the other hand, to be more realistic than their masters and mistresses[2] — as is Phénice here when she sounds a note of warning:

> Titus n'a point encore expliqué sa pensée.
> Rome vous voit, Madame, avec des yeux jaloux;
> La rigueur de ses lois m'épouvante pour vous:
> L'hymen chez les Romains n'admet qu'une Romaine;
> Rome hait tous les rois, et Bérénice est reine.
>
> (292-96)

Thus, Racine creates an atmosphere of expected joy for Bérénice at the end of the first act, but suggests that her optimism ('Le temps n'est plus, Phénice, où je pouvais trembler', l.297) might well be unfounded. By hinting at future misfortunes in this way, he creates suspense, and makes us anxious to see the new emperor and to discover the real nature of his intentions.

We are not made to wait long, since Racine opens Act II with Titus on stage. His sad demeanour (commented on by Paulin in line 336) makes us suspect that things are not going as well as Bérénice hopes; but his exact position is not made clear until after he has asked Paulin for his advice. This scene is fairly static and does not have any great intrinsic dramatic value. Its presence here is justified, however, by Racine's desire to ensure that we appreciate the very real pressures on Titus. The latter is, in theory, omnipotent; but Paulin, who has been chosen by the emperor because he represents the very best in Roman traditions (ll.351-66), points out at great length (ll.371-419) the strength of opposition to a marriage with a foreign queen. Julius Caesar,

---

[2] Arsace, on the other hand, is endowed with only limited insight. He consistently urges his master to entertain false hopes and is taken in by Bérénice's pretence about leaving Rome because she is offended.

who first subjected Rome, did not dare to marry Cleopatra. Mark Antony, although he did not marry her either, forgot his duty to Rome and paid the penalty ('Rome l'alla chercher jusques sur ses genoux'). Even wicked emperors like Caligula and Nero did not dare to infringe this one law (ll.387-402). How could Titus, who is desperate to be a good emperor (ll.1027-38), possibly begin his reign, therefore, by infringing Rome's most fundamental traditions? As he himself exclaims:

> Rome observe aujourd'hui ma conduite nouvelle.
> Quelle honte pour moi, quel présage pour elle,
> Si dès les premiers pas, renversant tous ses droits,
> Je fondais mon bonheur sur le débris des lois!
>
> (467-70)

A further advantage of the scene in question is that it enables us to witness the suffering which the separation will cause Titus in a situation in which he has no need to pretend that his feelings are other than they really are. Paulin would be only too happy to see the emperor wholeheartedly renounce his love, but in reply to his exhortation (not to say discreet threats), Titus can manage only an anguished lament: 'Hélas! à quel amour on veut que je renonce!' (l.420). A few lines later, when he is trying to make an announcement which will fill Paulin with joy (ll.491-98), he can hardly bear to pronounce the fateful words which will cause him as much emotional distress as they will to Bérénice:

> TITUS
> Je vais, Paulin...O ciel! puis-je le déclarer?
> PAULIN
> Quoi, Seigneur?
>
> TITUS
> Pour jamais je vais m'en séparer.
>
> (445-46)

It is obviously crucial that the spectacle of this suffering should be brought before us now since a man who promises a woman marriage for five years and then rejects her when he is finally free to put his promises into effect could easily be portrayed as a blackguard. A scenario based on the portrayal of Titus as villain and Bérénice as a totally innocent victim would be very melodramatic; but it would not satisfy Racine, who is attempting to win our sympathies for the emperor as well as for the queen.

It is particularly noteworthy in this respect that the technique used to confront Titus and Bérénice in Act II is the same as that utilized in Act I to confront Bérénice and Antiochus. The character who is in a difficult and (where Bérénice is concerned) unsuspected situation is presented first. This once again enables Racine to create a strong dramatic contrast between the sadness of the character who is on stage and the queen's joy as she sweeps in.

Her entry on this occasion is carefully timed by Racine to coincide with Titus's decision to commit himself blindly to his duty without reference to its emotional cost: 'Encore un coup, allons, il n'y faut plus penser./Je connais mon devoir, c'est à moi de le suivre:/Je n'examine point si j'y pourrai survivre' (ll.550-52). Though well-intentioned, such blind adherence to duty is not sufficient. It immediately breaks down when confronted by Bérénice's joy at seeing the emperor again. Her tone is apologetic ('Ne vous offensez pas si mon zèle indiscret/De votre solitude interrompt le secret'); but it is also gently reproachful: 'Vous êtes seul enfin, et ne me cherchez pas!' (ll.557-58, 566). Titus had despairingly hoped to compensate the queen for her loss by giving her additional kingdoms before sending her away; but this is unwittingly turned against him by the unsuspecting victim of his new-found sense of duty: 'Un soupir, un regard, un mot de votre bouche,/Voilà l'ambition d'un cœur comme le mien./Voyez-moi plus souvent, et ne me donnez rien' (ll.576-78). Her garrulousness clearly shows that, despite her rejection of Phénice's warning at the end of Act I, she is still alarmed by Titus's strange behaviour during the week since his father's death. Unfortunately, her search for reassurance only makes everyone's position worse. Knowing the nature of Titus's discussion with Paulin, the audience can feel him flinch as she repeatedly asks if he has been talking of her:

Mais parliez-vous de moi quand je vous ai surpris?
Dans vos discrets discours étais-je intéressée,
Seigneur? Etais-je au moins présente à la pensée?

(582-84)

We can understand, therefore, why his protestations of love are
so strained. Bérénice, however, cannot. Thus, the tremulous
expressions of sincere affection give way to anger and alarm:

Hé quoi! vous me jurez une éternelle ardeur,
Et vous me la jurez avec cette froideur?

(589-90)

This makes it even harder for Titus to speak to her. Worse still,
the queen assumes that Titus's distress is caused by his father's
recent death. Unaware of the irony, she urges him to forget his
sadness and commit himself to the government of Rome (ll.601-
04). She then compares his misunderstood sorrow to the distress
she experienced when Vespasian attempted to separate them:

Vous regrettez un père: hélas! faibles douleurs!
Et moi (ce souvenir me fait frémir encore)
On voulait m'arracher de tout ce que j'adore;
[...]
Moi, qui mourrais le jour qu'on voudrait m'interdire
De vous...

(610-16)

We have already been told that Titus has tried unsuccessfully to
tell Bérénice that she must leave (ll.471-82). His weakness now is
nothing new, therefore. On this occasion, however, we can *see*
why he finds it impossible to go through with his plan: unaware
of the fate which is about to befall her, Bérénice finds the very
words which will cut Titus to the quick. Titus is about to hurt
Bérénice without wishing to, while Bérénice is already hurting
him without being aware of it ('malgré lui et malgré elle').
Titus's pain is so great that he cuts the queen off in mid-
sentence before fleeing from the stage. This is psychologically

plausible; but it is also essential that Titus should not reveal his decision fully to Bérénice at this point. With such a limited plot, Racine cannot afford to precipitate the crisis too soon. Also, as far as the psychological realism of the play is concerned, Bérénice has to be *slowly* convinced of Titus's change of plan and then brought to the point where she can accept it. This is achieved not through one confrontation, but through three, of which this is only the first. Titus, for his part, has to be pushed to the end of his tether before his resolution to fulfil his duty can be put into effect.

Each stage of this process is handled with absolute mastery by Racine, as is his immediate problem at the end of Act II. Titus has not formally announced his decision to Bérénice; but he has said enough to make her suspect the cause of his distress, as she makes clear in her discussion with Phénice: 'N'est-ce point que de Rome il redoute la haine?/Il craint peut-être, il craint d'épouser une reine'. She is also aware of the gravity of the threat to her happiness if this is the case: 'Hélas! s'il était vrai...' (ll.639-41). We have already seen her close her mind, however, to Phénice's warning at the end of Act I. She does the same again now, anxiously searching for another reason which might explain Titus's apparent coldness. Skilfully linking sub-plot and main plot, Racine has her jump to the conclusion that the emperor must have heard of Antiochus's declaration of love and been offended thereby. This is plausible, but wrong. Crucially, we can see that Bérénice is *deliberately* failing to look any further: 'Ne cherchons point ailleurs le sujet [cause] de ma peine' (l.652). She fails to do so because this explanation stills her deep-seated fear that Titus might no longer love her (see below p.76). If Titus is jealous, she reassures herself, he must still be attached to her (ll.664-66). She is, in fact, right in believing that his feelings for her are as strong as ever; but, entranced as she is by her own infatuation with him, she wrongly assumes that, if her love is reciprocated, she can have nothing to fear from any other quarter (cf. l.298). This deliberate self-deception can only mean that her disillusionment will be even more of a shock when it comes. The increasing gloom and anxiety which this knowledge inspires in the audience makes us look forward to the next act with foreboding. At the same time, we experience a pressing desire to know what Titus will do now that he has tried to inform Bérénice of his decision and failed.

The answer comes at the beginning of Act III in a *coup de théâtre* which, when one sees or reads the play for the first time, comes as almost as much of a shock for the reader/spectator as for the character concerned: Titus turns in desperation to Antiochus, his unknown rival, and asks him to transmit the message to Bérénice and take her away with him! This creates massive dramatic irony, which the audience, having full knowledge of Antiochus's position, can appreciate only too well. It also causes, quite unintentionally, even more suffering for the poor Antiochus, who is forced into a position from which he would willingly escape if he could. He allows himself to hope that he might win the queen on the rebound, but only momentarily. Unlike Oreste, who is only too anxious to inform Hermione that she is spurned by Pyrrhus (*Andromaque*, II, 2), Antiochus realizes that he is the *last* person who should inform Bérénice of her misfortune (ll.833-48). His own suffering is increased still further, however, by the fact that, having just been prevented from leaving by Titus (III, 1), he is now prevented from doing so by Bérénice. The latter is in a very distressed state following Titus's behaviour in Act II, but she becomes even more distraught when, in the face of her reproaches, Antiochus cannot prevent himself from hinting that he has knowledge of something that he would rather not tell her (ll.858-70). It would be quite inappropriate to interpret this as a callous manœuvre on the part of Antiochus since he goes on to reveal his secret only when Bérénice threatens to hate him forever if he does not (ll.885-86). With the moral integrity which is one of his most striking characteristics, he does his best to soften the blow and even bears witness to Titus's sorrow at being forced to part from Bérénice (ll.896-902). Unfortunately for him, the news is simply too painful for her to accept. She blocks it from her mind, therefore, in the only way that she can think of — by accusing the innocent Antiochus of lying, and then banishing him from her sight:

Vous le souhaitez trop pour me persuader.
Non, je ne vous crois point. Mais, quoi qu'il en puisse
                                                                    [être,
Pour jamais à mes yeux gardez-vous de paraître.
                                                                    (914-16)

This unfair treatment does a lot, as we will see in a later chapter, to enhance the tragic stature of Antiochus at the expense (momentarily) of that of Bérénice. It is more important to note from our immediate point of view that Act III has advanced the plot only part of the way towards its natural conclusion. Bérénice's attack on Antiochus is no more than a desperate attempt to blind herself to the truth, as she herself admits as she asks Phénice to help her from the stage: 'Ne m'abandonne pas dans l'état où je suis./Hélas! pour me tromper je fais ce que je puis' (ll.917-18). To the extent that she is more aware of Titus's true intentions than she was at the end of Act II, the plot has advanced considerably. With her all-consuming love for Titus, however, Bérénice cannot accept that their liaison is at an end without hearing it from his own lips (cf. ll.1040-44; 1104-09). Thus, his rather cowardly decision to use Antiochus as a go-between ('Epargnez à mon cœur cet éclaircissement', l.742) does not finally fulfil its purpose. The unwilling Titus will be forced to confront Bérénice again.

I wish to analyse the confrontation concerned, and the monologue by Titus which precedes it, in some detail in the next two chapters. I shall restrict myself here, therefore, to general comments about the way in which these scenes are prepared and their role in the general economy of the plot.

One of the most striking things about the second confrontation between Titus and Bérénice is that it is preceded by monologues by both characters. Bérénice is on stage in Act IV scene 1, anxiously awaiting the return of Phénice, who has been sent to beg Titus to see her. When the emperor arrives, he is accompanied by his retinue, and the dishevelled and distraught Bérénice is persuaded to withdraw into her apartment to await him there. Titus, for his part, requires time in which to think before facing the queen; and he also needs to think alone. He dismisses his followers, therefore, and sends Paulin in to see the queen in the hope that he might be able to calm her while Titus attempts to build up his resolve.

The ensuing confrontation differs in this way from the confrontations in Act I and Act II. In each of those cases, we were introduced to the suffering character on stage (Antiochus, Titus) before he was brought face to face with Bérénice. Racine will obviously have wanted to vary his technique on this occasion; but he also had intrinsically important reasons for doing so. Not the least substantial of these was his desire (*pace* Weinberg, *32*, p.157) to make sure that the audience's sympathies are shared by *both* the main characters. Titus's anguish both during his monologue and during the confrontation is only too apparent. Bérénice, on the other hand, taunts the emperor with cruel allegations which we, like the emperor, know to be unfair:

BERENICE
Vous ne comptez pour rien les pleurs de Bérénice.
TITUS
Je les compte pour rien! Ah! ciel! quelle injustice!
(1147-48)

I will argue later that Racine is deliberately playing a game of brinkmanship by substantially reducing the queen's tragic stature before dramatically restoring it in the closing scene of the play. It is important to note now, on the other hand, that he deliberately focuses our attention on her distress at the beginning of Act IV in order to remind us that, however bitter or unjust she may be, her cruelty to Titus is caused by her own deep distress.

A further advantage of Racine's technique on this occasion is that it adds an entirely new dimension to Titus's plight. When he imagines the confrontation which awaits him and asks himself whether he will really be able to tell Bérénice the truth, his vivid questions ('Soutiendrai-je ces yeux dont la douce langueur/Sait si bien découvrir les chemins de mon cœur?', ll.993-94) are given added weight by the fact that we know that Bérénice is just the other side of the door through which she has just fled. His questions are, moreover, endowed with marked irony in that he is still remembering the tender Bérénice whom he faced at the beginning of Act II scene 4. We, however, have seen the cruel way in which she has just treated Antiochus, as well as her desire to subject Titus to her 'juste fureur' (l.961).

By having the queen leave the stage somewhat unwillingly in scene 2 (she is anxious to see Titus as soon as possible, and, unlike Phénice, would quite like him to see her in a distressed state, l.972), Racine is also able to prepare the highly dramatic moment when, just as Titus manages to convince himself that he must send Bérénice away (l.1040), the queen bursts in. The contrast with her entry in Act II, when she was announced by Rutile, could not be greater. On that occasion, the advance warning gave the suffering emperor a chance to waver (ll.553-54). This time, Titus has done his best to convince himself that Bérénice should be allowed to stay, but has been forced to recognize that this is impossible (see below, chapter 3). His resolve remains firm, therefore, even in the face of her unexpected arrival. Whereas Bérénice is brought up short by his obviously unexpected presence right outside her door (l.1042), Titus at last finds the strength to tell her that she must depart: 'Car enfin, ma princesse, il faut nous séparer' (l.1061).

In this way, the truth is finally revealed to Bérénice by Titus himself after a long process of understandable but none the less cruel evasion, which has occupied the best part of four acts.[3] It seems, therefore, as if the rest of the play will conform to a pattern highlighted by H.T. Barnwell, who rightly argues that Racine often writes plays in which the plot is 'virtually completed in a dénouement at the end of the fourth act', Act V being left free for the characters' tragic self-discovery as they are brought 'face to face with the reality of what they have done and of what they are' (9, p.234. Cf. ibid., pp.208-09). Titus's monologue in Act IV scene 4 is certainly a key point in the play since it shows him, for the first and only time, attempting to convince himself that he is not duty-bound to send Bérénice away. His rejection of the tempting but fundamentally

---

[3] Titus has been trying unsuccessfully to inform Bérénice of his change of heart for over a week (ll.471-76).

misconceived belief that Rome might be won over by Bérénice's virtues or by the intensity of her love for him (ll.1007-13) proves once and for all that there is no escape that way. Titus's main problem throughout the play, however, is not to convince himself of where his duty lies (he knows that, as we have seen, when the play opens). His problem is his inability to see Bérénice suffer; and this problem returns, in an even more acute form, *after* he has told her that she must leave Rome. He begins to weaken, indeed, in Act IV scene 5 when, renouncing the longed-for marriage, the queen humiliates herself by asking if she might be permitted to remain in Rome, eliciting the sad but affirmative reply from her unwilling interlocutor: 'Hélas! vous pouvez tout, Madame. Demeurez:/Je n'y résiste point' (ll.1130-31).

This concession comes to nothing because Bérénice is offended by his evident reluctance to agree and, following an exchange of arguments which I will analyse in chapter 4, herself insists on going. This might appear to provide the emperor with a solution to his problems; but it does not, since Bérénice cannot face being rejected by the man she loves and resolves to commit suicide (ll.1185-97). This is the one 'solution' to his problem that Titus *cannot* accept — he informs Paulin, the very incarnation of his normal devotion to duty: 'Paulin, je suis perdu, je n'y pourrai survivre./La reine veut mourir. Allons, il faut la suivre./Courons à son secours (ll.1199-1201). So great is his torment, indeed, that he spurns Rome itself, accusing it of being a barbarous city which simply does not merit that such a queen should lose her life:

> Non, je suis un barbare;
> Moi-même je me hais. Néron, tant détesté,
> N'a point à cet excès poussé sa cruauté.
> Je ne souffrirai point que Bérénice expire.
> Allons, Rome en dira ce qu'elle en voudra dire.
>
> (1212-16)

In this way, Titus is not only thrown back into his earlier quandary: he is put in a very much worse situation in which his moral and emotional dilemma is intensified by the unacceptable prospect of the queen's suicide.

It is no coincidence that it is at this point in the play that Racine chooses to provide the spatial symbolism of the emperor's tragic problem analysed in chapter 1 (p.x). The whole pace of the drama, which at the beginning of the act was too slow for the impatient Bérénice (ll.953-54) is also speeded up as the disorientated Titus ('Moi-même en ce moment sais-je si je respire?', l.1240) is exhorted to follow two conflicting policies at the same time. His decision to meet the Roman senators first gives no clear clue as to the nature of his decision since he tells Antiochus that he will return and demonstrate how much he loves Bérénice (ll.1253-54). Far from resolving Titus's problems at the end of Act IV and leaving Act V for the tragic recognition of the consequences of his decision, Racine is deliberately increasing his, and our, uncertainty so that the level of the suspense can be raised to a paroxysm of intensity at the end of the penultimate act.

B. Weinberg has argued that Antiochus's role is already over-extended in the earlier part of the play and that it becomes more irrelevant still at the beginning of Act V (*32*, pp.154-56). He has failed to realize, however, that Racine is well aware that we are anxious to see Titus and Bérénice in order that our doubts concerning their decisions may be resolved. By concentrating on Antiochus and Arsace in scenes 1-4, the playwright prolongs the suspense created at the end of the previous act.

With the brilliant economy which Odette de Mourgues has dubbed the 'triumph of relevance' (*24*), he also exploits these apparently inconsequential scenes in another way. Although not directly involved in the main plot, Arsace gives us news of it when he joyfully announces to his master that, apparently offended by Titus's delay in coming to see her, Bérénice has decided to leave Rome (ll.1265-69). This apparent change of heart comes as a surprise both to Antiochus (l.1269) and to the audience, which has seen that the queen's love for Titus is greater than her pride.[4] Even Antiochus, who would like to

---

[4] Bérénice's pride can make itself felt when she believes that there is no hope of winning Titus (ll.1179-80); but she is quite prepared to humiliate herself by offering to remain in Rome without marrying him (ll.1126-29).

believe it, dares not fully do so (ll.1279-84). It would be wrong, therefore, to present it as a real *coup de théâtre*. It does, however, augment the suspense: could it be, we ask, that Racine is going to settle for such a lame and psychologically unrealistic dénouement? The answer, as we will soon discover, is 'no'. Racine is preparing the ground for a very different and much more dramatic ending. Arsace has got his facts right, but his interpretation wrong. Bérénice's real intentions are, as we have already noted, to escape from the surveillance of the attendants whom Titus has ordered to keep watch over her. The letter to which Arsace refers ('elle écrit à César', l.1269) is a suicide note which the emperor is to receive only when it is too late.

A further advantage of Arsace's erroneous interpretation of the queen's behaviour is that it serves to exacerbate the atmosphere of tension and uncertainty which has been reigning since the end of Act IV. Antiochus is lucid enough to realize that his hopes of winning Bérénice are still slim, but his anguish is so great that he appears to have forgotten Titus's promise to return in order to see Bérénice. Lines 1291-92 ('Venez, Prince, venez. Je veux bien que vous-même/Pour la dernière fois vous voyez si je l'aime') closely echo lines 1253-54 ('Voyez la reine. Allez. J'espère à mon retour/Qu'elle ne pourra plus douter de mon amour'); but they seem to come as a bolt from the blue for the forlorn lover, who laments the way in which his tentative hopes have been so quickly dashed. Resolving on suicide, he flees from the sight of Titus and Bérénice, who enter the stage just as he leaves (ll.1293-1302). His understandable failure to obey the emperor's summons will be skilfully exploited by Racine, who will have Titus call him back to the stage so that, however unwillingly, he can both witness and help to provoke the play's dénouement.

The third confrontation between Titus and Bérénice will make this dénouement possible; but, as it begins, it hardly seems likely to do so. Whereas Bérénice was only too anxious to see Titus in Act II (so that he could reassure her) and again in Act IV (so that she could force him to tell her the truth), she is now determined to flee from his presence.[5] She is prevented from doing so, but

[5] Racine is unable to provide Antiochus with a credible reason for returning to

there is a dramatic reversal of roles. In Act IV, Bérénice was the supplicant, while Titus made unwilling concessions. Now, it is the other way around. The queen, who had been so garrulous in Act II, is so deeply hurt by what she regards as the emperor's betrayal of her love that she is most unwilling to speak to him. She also has a secret (the fact that she is leaving Rome only to commit suicide). Understandably, therefore, she gives the emperor only curt replies in lines 1307 and 1308. Titus, on the other hand, pleads with her to listen to him (ibid.). Whereas she wishes to escape from Rome in order to avoid hearing the 'peuple injurieux/Qui fait de [son] malheur retentir tous ces lieux' (ll.1313-14), Titus (who was ready to sacrifice his own and Bérénice's happiness in order to rule this people well) suggests that she is wrong to pay it any attention: 'Ecoutez-vous, Madame, une foule insensée?' (l.1319). Having told the queen in their confrontation in Act IV that she must go, he now pleads with her to stay (l.1312).

The about-turn in his attitudes makes it seem as if Antiochus is right to believe that the emperor now wishes to be reconciled with the queen. His words do not reflect a considered decision, however. As Titus explains to Bérénice later, he came to see her in despair. He was certainly motivated by his love for her, but he had no idea of what he ought to do:

> Je suis venu vers vous sans savoir mon dessein:
> Mon amour m'entraînait; et je venais peut-être
> Pour me chercher moi-même et pour me reconnaître.
>
> (1382-84)

The fact that he weakens now is the result both of his own suffering — which he feels, for the first time, exceeds that of Bérénice (ll.1289-90) — and his dismay at finding such a change in the woman he loves (l.1385).

Titus's use of the word 'Demeurez' in line 1312 might suggest that he has fallen back on the compromise solution suggested by

the antechamber in Act V (see ll.1260-61); but brilliantly exploits the unity of place by making Bérénice rush on to the stage in a despairing attempt at avoiding a confrontation with Titus, who has come to see her in her apartment.

Bérénice in Act IV, when, in reply to her request that she be allowed to remain in Rome without marrying him, he answered: 'Hélas! vous pouvez tout, Madame. *Demeurez*' (l.1130). Racine, however, does not find it necessary to be precise about Titus's suggestion, which is soon to be withdrawn anyway. The important thing from the point of view of the playwright's dramatic strategy is to deliberately undo most of the progress made by the plot hitherto. Titus had been trying to tell Bérénice to go for eight days before the play opened (ll.471-76); he confirms his decision to do so in Act II scene 2; his courage having failed him in the ensuing confrontation with Bérénice, he uses Antiochus as a go-between in Act III, before finally finding the resolve necessary to acquaint the queen with her misfortune with his own lips in Act IV scene 5. Even if he is now offering no more than to return to the compromise solution suggested by her on the latter occasion, the situation has still been radically transformed in that it is now *Titus himself* who is suggesting this inadequate way out. By weakening Titus's resolve in this way, Racine is preparing the ground for two peripeteias, which, following each other in the brief period before the final curtain, will not only reverse Titus's most recent decision but also persuade Bérénice that she must agree to go. Her unexpected decision to comply with the emperor's wishes then provides a final, even more dramatic, *coup de théâtre* on which the play can close.

The first of these peripeteias is provided by the letter mentioned by Arsace. Bérénice has it in her hands as, fleeing from Titus, she re-enters the antechamber at the beginning of scene 5. The emperor is so occupied with trying to get Bérénice to listen to him and defending himself from her accusations that he pays it no attention at first. But, getting the worst of the argument, he tries to take refuge from her bitterly ironic onslaught in lines 1345-49 by snatching it from her. Having been taken in, like Arsace, by her pretended desire to leave Rome because her pride has been hurt by the behaviour of the populace, he is now shocked by what he reads. Yet he is also galvanized enough by it to interpose himself between the fleeing Bérénice and the door (l.1358). The sudden change of roles between the two characters is amply symbolized by the way in which, once again acting as emperor, Titus summons the absent Antiochus, whilst Bérénice, whose manœuvre has now been prematurely exposed, sinks into a chair (ll.1358-62).

Titus ought not to have been taken in by the queen's deception since she had always made it quite clear that she could not live without him (cf. ll.615-16). She had, furthermore, threatened suicide in explicit terms in Act IV (ll.1185-97), and was subsequently described by Antiochus as seeking the means to put her threat into effect (l.1230). That, however, was when she was still under the shock of Titus's bombshell. What alarms him now is the fact that her plan to escape from Rome and then commit suicide is premeditated and will obviously be put into effect unless he can dissuade her. On realizing this, Titus, who had always known that sending Bérénice away would be difficult (ll.1363 ff.), finds that his pain exceeds his worst fears (ll.1385-88).

In the depths of despair, he suddenly finds the lucidity to appraise his situation correctly. Marriage to Bérénice is rejected as incompatible with his duty (ll.1391-96). And abdication is excluded because it would mean behaving in a way which would make him unworthy of the woman who has inspired him with his new-found sense of duty (see below p.69). The compromise solution (allowing Bérénice to remain in Rome without marrying her) is not mentioned, possibly because it would put her in the humiliating position he has just ruled out for himself, or (more probably) because Titus is anxious to present their situation in terms of clearly articulated contrasts of which only one (sending Bérénice away and remaining to rule undistracted) could possibly be acceptable. It is certainly the only possibility that he is prepared to consider. Abandoning all attempts at convincing Bérénice of the inescapability of his duty, therefore, he counters her plans to commit suicide by threatening to take his own life unless she agrees both to leave Rome and to remain alive:

Si vos pleurs plus longtemps viennent frapper ma vue,
Si toujours à mourir je vous vois résolue,
S'il faut qu'à tous moments je tremble pour vos jours,

Si vous ne me jurez d'en respecter le cours,
Madame, à d'autres pleurs vous devez vous attendre:
En l'état où je suis je puis tout entreprendre,
Et je ne réponds pas que ma main à vos yeux
N'ensanglante à la fin nos funestes adieux.

(1415-22)

Titus's statement of his position is neither completely new (he had overcome the temptation to believe that he could escape from his duty in Act IV scene 4) nor completely rational (a dead emperor would be in no better position to rule than one who had abdicated). It does, however, present the queen with a new threat which is so vehemently expressed that it cannot but be sincere.[6] This threat and the suffering which has prompted it obviously move Bérénice (see l.1483). The whole transformation in her position has, however, been too rapid for her to respond fully. All that she can manage at the moment is an anguished 'Hélas!' (l.1423).

Before she can make her final renunciation, a second impetus is required. This is provided by Antiochus, who, summoned by Titus in line 1291 and again in line 1362, finally enters at line 1425. The double summons was necessary because Antiochus, driven to distraction by the continual ups and downs of his hopeless fate, wanted to commit suicide (ll.1299-1302). He still wishes to do so (ll.1458-59); but his character has been given a new dynamism by his decision to reveal to Titus his secret love for Bérénice. His hopes of winning her have never been anything but slight, but it is only now that, having seen her distress when rejected by Titus, he realizes that he stands no chance of being loved by her even if she were rejected by the emperor (ll.1447-49). Unable to overcome his love for her except through death, he offers his life as a sacrifice to the gods in the hope that they will protect both Bérénice and the man that she loves (ll.1463-68).

This act of self-abnegation is all the more moving because it is

[6] France and Weinberg express doubts about the sincerity of Titus's suicide threat (*14*, p.226; *32*, p.153). Failure to accept that frustrated love can lead to a genuine desire for death will, however, rob the play of much of its tragic potential. See below pp.72, 76-77.

based on a false premiss: the belief that Titus and Bérénice have
been reconciled and that it is Antiochus himself who has finally
confirmed the hopelessness of his situation by bringing them
back together (ll.1451-62). Antiochus is, of course, wrong in
believing this, but Bérénice is none the less moved by the
spectacle of the distress which she has been causing (ll.1469-74).
Titus, who was in full flow when Antiochus interrupted him, is
struck dumb by his revelation; but Bérénice, who was almost
mute, suddenly finds the energy to rise and prevent both men
from going through with their threats. She reminds Titus that
she has never desired anything but his love (ll.1475-79) and
refers to the distress which she experienced when she thought
that his love for her was dead (ll.1480-81). She now realizes that
the suffering he has manifested in threatening to commit suicide
is proof of the genuineness of his affection (ll.1482-83). Secure
in this knowledge, she can make the same sacrifice that he is
making in the interests of the Roman empire (ll.1484-88), and,
indeed, make what is for her an even greater sacrifice — she will
refrain from committing suicide even though her life from now
on will be a living death:

> Ce n'est pas tout: je veux, en ce moment funeste,
> Par un dernier effort couronner tout le reste:
> Je vivrai, je suivrai vos ordres absolus.
> Adieu, Seigneur. Régnez; je ne vous verrai plus.
>
> (1491-94)

Endowed with the renewed moral stature which this effort of
understanding and self-control brings her, she can turn to
Antiochus, the man whom she has most cruelly wronged. She
explains, kindly, that she cannot love him, and then demands of
him the same sacrifice that she is making herself: that he remain
alive (ll.1495-99). With complete presence of mind, she asks him
to delay his departure until after she has gone, before addressing
a final farewell to Titus. The theatre is hushed; Titus is too
stunned to speak; and only Antiochus can manage a strangled
'Hélas!' (l.1506). The leitmotif of sadness, which has run right

through the play,[7] reaches its climax as all three protagonists realize that there will be no escape from their anguish.

The tragic consequences of this dénouement will require analysis in a later chapter. It should be evident now, however, that, far from organizing his plot so that it falls into two parts with the climax of the first occurring towards the end of Act IV with Act V being given over to the exploration of the consequences thereof, Racine has deliberately delayed the resolution of the problem faced by Titus and Bérénice until the closing scene of the play. It is a moral certainty that he did so, in part at least, in order to answer the critics who had claimed that the latter part of Act V in *Britannicus* was not essential to the plot.[8] But his main purpose was, in all probability, to ensure that his apparently unpromising material was rendered as dramatic as possible. The touchy and often arrogant Racine was, for once, being unduly modest when, speaking of Bérénice's climactic leave-taking, he claimed:

le dernier adieu qu'elle dit à Titus, et l'effort qu'elle se fait pour s'en séparer n'est pas le moins tragique de la pièce; et j'ose dire qu'il renouvelle assez bien dans le cœur des spectateurs l'émotion que le reste y avait pu exciter.

(Preface, p.27)

---

[7] See, for example, lines 159, 199, 224 ('douleur', 'malheur'); 158, 237, 336 ('tristesse'); 152, 157, 202 ('larmes', 'pleurs'). The suicide threats of the three protagonists are the culmination of a constant preoccupation with death. See lines 34, 501, 552, 751-56, 975-56, 1100, 1122-25, 1186-93, 1200, 1227-32, 1385, 1407-22, 1459-68.

[8] See the first preface to the play: ' "Tout cela est inutile, disent mes censeurs: la pièce est finie au récit de la mort de Britannicus, et l'on ne devrait point écouter le reste" '.

3. The Monologue

We have seen in the preceding chapter that Racine bases his plot on a constant oscillation between firmness and weakness on the part of Titus, and between blindness and understanding on the part of Bérénice. These oscillations are presented in a dynamic way so that the play reaches a dramatic, and unexpected, climax in Act V. If we now look at the overall structure of *Bérénice*, we can see that each act is based on a confrontation between two of the three main characters:-

Act I:	Antiochus and Bérénice
Act II:	Titus and Bérénice
Act III:	Antiochus and Bérénice
Act IV:	Titus and Bérénice
Act V:	Titus and Bérénice

This series of confrontations is dominated, for obvious reasons, by the meetings between the emperor and the queen, who face each other three times. It is complicated, however, in Act III and Act V. In the earlier of these two acts, Titus's inability to face Bérénice is symbolized by Antiochus's role as go-between: he sees both protagonists, but separately. In the final act, he is again used symbolically: as an outsider who is brought back in at a moment when the confrontation between Titus and the queen is about to reach its final turning point. His vehement words as he enters (he cuts Titus off in the middle of line 1429) also help to bring the play to its febrile climax, previously prepared by the large number of short scenes at the end of Act IV (scenes 6-8), [9] and at the beginning of Act V (scenes 1-4).

The confusion reigning at this point of the play is further highlighted by the way in which Racine handles Antiochus's exit in Act V scene 4. Determined not to suffer any more, the

[9] The original edition (1671) contained a ninth scene which was later suppressed.

tormented friend and suitor utters a cry of anguish as he sees the two lovers re-entering in line 1301 ('Bérénice! Titus!') and flees from their presence. This leaves the stage momentarily empty in a way which was criticized by the Abbé de Villars (see *41*, p.253). Had he been trying to understand the play rather than to make criticisms for criticism's sake, he would have noticed that Racine had deliberately departed from the normal *liaison des scènes* (in which at least one character remains on stage) so that he could emphasize the disorder which has to reach a peak towards the close of the play. This prepares a dramatic contrast with the calm self-control suddenly established by Bérénice in the closing scene.

It is hoped that the preceding analysis will have convinced the reader that, though his material was deliberately limited, Racine exploited it in such a way that Daniel Mornet is quite wrong when he describes *Bérénice* as 'une pièce peu dramatique' (quoted in *3*, p.33 n.5). I would like now to leave the overall development of the plot in order to examine some of the ways in which Racine develops individual scenes. The scenes chosen for analysis are Titus's monologue in Act IV scene 4 and the ensuing confrontation with Bérénice in scene 5.

The first of these scenes merits detailed examination for several reasons. Thematically, it is crucial since it is the only occasion when Titus tries to convince himself that marrying Bérénice is not incompatible with his duty. This has an important effect on our sympathies for the emperor (it shows that he would escape from his duty if he felt that he honourably could), and also prepares the dénouement: it is because we have seen the emperor fail in his efforts to convince himself that Bérénice may stay that we can understand his instinctive refusal to marry her at the end of Act V. From the dramatic point of view, the scene in question also highlights the problems posed by Racine's decision to 'faire quelque chose de rien': having one character alone on the stage is not, unless skilfully handled, the most effective of devices. Titus's monologue presents, too, a suitably circumscribed opportunity to examine an essential feature of all of Racine's plays: the way in which he makes his style reflect his characters' inner torments.

The emperor's anguish is apparent from the fact that he needs, literally, to take counsel with himself before facing Bérénice (ll.987-98); but it becomes more obvious still when, in the middle of the passage (ll.1000-13), we find him vainly but enthusiastically trying to convince himself that she should be allowed to stay. From this point of view, Titus's monologue may be regarded as symbolizing the victory of duty over love. Although Titus is only too keen to succumb to his own wishful-thinking, he quickly becomes aware of the harsh realities of his situation: 'Rome jugea ta reine en condamnant ses rois' (l.1017). It is important to realize, however, that the emotional involvement which makes him try to blind himself to the truth remains just as great when he has decided that he has no alternative but to send the queen away. Although aware of his duty, he finds it necessary, indeed, to apply as much psychological pressure to himself as possible before he can summon up the determination required to put his good intentions into effect. This is why he *continues* to present an equally false, though different, picture of his predicament. His answer to his own despairing question in line 1030 ('Qu'ai-je fait pour l'honneur? J'ai tout fait pour l'amour') is true in the sense that his sorrow has paralysed him since his accession (ll.471-76); but, as Bérénice herself laments (ll.151-58), he can hardly be said to have devoted the past eight days to his love for her. Titus is deceiving himself, too, when he tries to augment his sense of guilt by implying that his main reason for wishing to be emperor was to rule well (ll.1037-38). He did wish to be a good emperor, but his principal desire seems to have been to marry Bérénice and make her empress (ll.435-38). I have highlighted these subtle distortions of the truth as a warning to the reader, who should note that what a Racinian character says about himself (or herself) is not always a reliable guide. It is also important that we should note that, though Titus overcomes the temptation to escape into wishful thinking, he never reaches the stage where he can take an objective view of his dilemma and find a fully rational solution to it. Had he managed to do so, he might well have been able to stand firm in his confrontation with Bérénice in Act IV scene 5. As it is, his hard-won resolve abandons him in the face of her reproaches and pleas to be allowed to stay (see below chapter 4).

Confirmation of the emperor's continuing distraction is provided by the fact that the rhetorical techniques used to express his anguish (antitheses, exclamations, questions, imperatives, repetition) are just as frequent in the later part of the passage when the full force of his duty has impressed itself on him as they are in the earlier part when he finds that duty hard to face.

Before I comment on the rhetorical tropes concerned, it is necessary to say something about the function of rhetoric in Racine's plays. Although interest in rhetoric has grown enormously in recent years, many students are still unfamiliar with it when they come to study Racine for the first time. Those who do have some knowledge of it tend to equate it with persuasion and/or with ostentatious verbal display, and find much in *Bérénice* to confirm such a view. Titus, for instance, is clearly being subjected to persuasive rhetoric by Paulin in Act II scene 2. Likewise, he is trying to persuade Bérénice in his long speech in Act V scene 6, and, indeed, to persuade *himself*, in the second half of his monologue in Act IV, that he must send the queen away. There is also evidence to show that seventeenth-century actors regarded such tirades and monologues as bravura pieces giving them a chance to display their oratorical skills. That Racine would not have been totally averse to this is shown both by his proud reference to the 'élégance de l'expression' of the play and by his much earlier decision to have his plays performed by the actors of the Hôtel de Bourgogne rather than by Molière's troupe, which performed tragedies in a much less stylized way (*33*, pp.1-2, 31). It would be wrong, however, to assume that Racine's rhetoric is *only* persuasive, or that it is *only* intended for display. Its main function is both to express the emotions of the character speaking (thereby delineating his or her character) and to help the audience respond to those emotions. This is the true purpose of the rhetorical figures mentioned above. They help us understand Titus's mind as he contemplates the true extent of his dilemma and then moves from self-doubt through fear, anguish, surprise, self-delusion, lucidity, self-laceration and despair to his final determination to send Bérénice away. It is the spectacle of these constantly changing and vividly expressed emotions which makes the scene dramatic and, of course, increases our sympathy for the tormented emperor.

Antithesis is one of the most obvious of the figures used by Racine to highlight the situation in which the emperor finds himself. It is a natural technique for him to use since Titus is caught between his love and his duty. As he tries to wrest himself free from his dilemma, he deliberately highlights the opposition between his feelings for Bérénice and his duty to the empire:

> Ah! lâche, fais l'amour, et renonce à l'empire,
> Au bout de l'univers va, cours te confiner.
>
> (1024-25)

The spatial antithesis (Rome *versus* the ends of the earth) reinforces the love/duty antithesis and intensifies the emperor's sense of shame. This reinforcement is required because Titus is only too aware of the pain he will inflict on a woman who loves him: 'Je viens percer un cœur qui m'adore, qui m'aime' (l.999). This pain will be so great that Titus's awareness of it actually begins to undermine his moral values. Although he always tries to live up to the highest traditions of Roman constancy, he wonders if this stoic virtue is not really an unacceptable vice: 'C'est peu d'être constant, il faut être barbare' (l.992).

The balance here between the two equal halves of the lines (hemistichs) throws the two contrasting adjectives into relief and amply highlights the emperor's ability to sympathize in advance with the anguish of the woman on whom he is about to inflict so much suffering. The dominant antitheses of the monologue emphasize a different aspect of his problem, however. As he contemplates the effects of the announcement which will pierce Bérénice to the heart, Titus suddenly wonders why he should do such a thing and realizes, equally suddenly, that *he* is the author of his own misfortune: 'Et pourquoi le percer? Qui l'ordonne? Moi-même' (l.1000). This awful paradox is, as we will see in a later chapter, at the very heart of the emperor's tragic problem.

During this monologue, however, he eagerly attempts to escape from the trap in which he finds himself by concentrating on a series of antitheses which all suggest that there is a way out of his problem. Deliberately forgetting what Paulin has told him about the strength of Roman opinion (ll.371-419), he tries to profit from the fact that the palace is not actually surrounded by a protesting mob in order to suggest that there is no resistance to the marriage: 'Car enfin Rome a-t-elle *expliqué* ses souhaits?/ *L'entendons-nous crier* autour de ce palais?' (ll.1001-02). The question is rhetorical and prepares Titus's own wilfully blind answer: 'Tout *se tait*' (l.1005). At the same time, he also highlights the alleged indifference of everyone around him ('*Tout* se tait') in order to underline his supposed folly in causing his own unhappiness: 'et *moi seul*, trop prompt à me troubler,/J'avance des malheurs que je puis reculer' (ll.1005-06). Half recognizing even now that the problem is too serious to be ignored in this way, he accuses himself of bringing misfortunes down on his head which could at least be postponed: '*J'avance* des malheurs *que je puis reculer*'. The density of these interwoven antitheses at this point in the text is no accident. The emperor knows where his real problem lies, and has put all his inventive powers at the service of his emotions in order to try to prove to himself that it may be circumvented or at least postponed.

Racine also makes Titus's sufferings evident in less subtle but equally important ways: by using apostrophes and exclamations, for example. The emperor's self-doubt is apparent when he addresses himself as 'téméraire' (l.988), as are his disdain for his own weakness when he calls himself 'lâche' (l.1024) and his despair at having wasted precious time when he asks how long he has to live and then exclaims: 'Et, de ce peu de jours si longtemps attendus,/Ah! malheureux! combien j'en ai déjà perdus!' (ll.1037-38). There are other exclamations in line 987 as he tries to summon up the strength to face the distraught Bérénice ('Hé bien') and in line 1024 when he upbraids himself for his cowardice ('Ah!').

Exclamation is a very natural figure to find in the mouth of a man who is subject to so much distress. The reader should note, on the other hand, that exclamations are by no means as numerous as one might have expected either here in the emperor's monologue or in the next scene during his argument with Bérénice. This tells us something quite crucial about the way in which Racine, who in this provides an exact parallel with his contemporaries, uses rhetoric in order to render anguish, anger or despair. When experiencing such emotions, many of us tend to become inarticulate. So, too, at times, do Racine's characters. The end of Act II scene 4 is a good example. Titus, though trying to inform Bérénice of his decision, is unable to do so and breaks off with a despairing 'Mais...'. The queen orders him to continue in two separate replies ('Achevez...', 'Parlez'), but he can only manage an anguished 'Hélas!' and then stutter: 'Rome...L'Empire...'. Significantly, however, all these dis-jointed exchanges will, when put together, form a single alex-andrine (l.623) — the twelve-syllable line which was deemed most suitable for an elevated genre like tragedy.[10] This is a perfect example of the way in which Racine and contemporary tragedians sought to render disorder. The disorder had to be conveyed if the play was to be 'realistic' and to move the audience. But it had to be conveyed in a way which was artistically satisfying. The compromise arrived at was known as 'le beau désordre' (*14*, pp.27-28, 34, 178-79).

This 'beau désordre' is particularly apparent in the way in which Racine articulates Titus's monologue. He is clearly anxious to convey the impression of a racing mind, working at frantic pace as it seeks to find a solution to a terrible problem; but he also imposes a clearly defined order on it such that it can be divided into its component parts. There are three main sections. The first extends from line 987 to 999, in which Titus asks himself whether he has the courage (or cruelty) required to send Bérénice away. In the second section (ll.1000-13), he begins to wonder whether he really has to do so, his doubts forming three subsections. In line 1000, he asks who is forcing him to pierce her heart and answers incredulously: 'Moi-même'. In

[10] Alexandrines were regarded as the equivalent of prose. The *stances* used by Corneille in *Le Cid* (I, 6) were regarded as poetry and condemned as unrealistic. This is a matter of pure convention. See *14*, pp.32-33.

lines 1001-06, he reinforces his doubts by pointing out that Rome has not yet formally expressed its disapproval of the longed-for match. Then, in lines 1007-13, he goes further as, letting himself be carried away by wishful-thinking, he hopes that, if the Romans take the queen's love and sufferings into account, they will actually favour the marriage. The third section extends from line 1013 until the end of the speech, and contains four subsections. In the first (ll.1013-23), the emperor's lucidity returns as, becoming aware of his attempt to delude himself, he remembers Rome's implacable hostility towards kings and queens. In the second (ll.1024-26), he chastizes himself for his weakness, which, he feels, makes him unworthy to rule. In the third section (ll.1027-38), he laments the time he has wasted since his father's death, time which should have been devoted to making his subjects happy rather than to thinking about Bérénice. In the final subsection (ll.1039-40), he at last confirms his decision to tell her that she must go.

It is easier, of course, to identify these divisions and subdivisions when reading the text than when listening to it in the theatre. A skilful actor will, however, attempt to make them clear as he tries to follow Titus's train of thought. Two of the turning points are so obvious that they cannot be missed. The first occurs at line 1000 as Titus picks up the verb 'percer' from the previous line ('Je viens percer un cœur qui m'adore') and asks himself why he should do so: 'Et pourquoi le percer?' The second turning point is more evident still since, availing himself of a technique which is effective precisely because he utilizes it so sparingly, Racine places it in the middle of line 1013. Having reached a climax of enthusiastic but illusory hope in the first hemistich ('Rome sera pour nous...'), the emperor suddenly crashes back to earth in the remaining half of the line: 'Titus, ouvre les yeux!' The fact that Titus's monologue contains these obvious twists and turns shows that, although carefully structured, it is not intended to appear monolithic. The aesthetically satisfying impression of varied order (or orderly variety) which it creates is increased by the way in which Racine distributes Titus's frequent questions.

Questions are, as one would expect in a scene in which a

character is subject to paroxysms of self-doubt, extremely numerous: 29 in 52 lines. They are not, however, spread evenly through the text: Racine groups them in ways which accentuate the movement of the emperor's mind. The first cluster occurs, naturally enough, at the beginning of the passage as Titus asks himself if he has the courage to face the queen. His first questions are short, but they gradually accelerate as he moves from self-doubt to self-accusation:

Hé bien, Titus, que viens-tu faire?	(2+2/1+3)
Bérénice t'attend. Où viens-tu, téméraire?	(3+3/1+5)
Tes adieux sont-ils prêts? T'es-tu bien consulté?	(3+3/3+3)
Ton cœur te promet-il assez de cruauté?	(2+4/2+4)

The questions then become longer, running into two and then three lines as Titus emphasizes the difficulty of the struggle ahead:

Soutiendrai-je ces yeux dont la douce langueur
Sait si bien découvrir les chemins de mon cœur?
Quand je verrai ces yeux armés de tous leurs charmes,
Attachés sur les miens, m'accabler de leur larmes,
Me souviendrai-je alors de mon triste devoir?

                                        (993-97)

The build-up through lines 995-96 to the stressed 'alors' of line 997 emphasizes the emperor's awareness of the difference between deciding in the abstract that Bérénice must go and actually telling her so to her face. The enormity of the problem is further underlined by a one-line question in which brevity emphasizes the poignancy of the situation: 'Pourrai-je dire enfin: "Je ne veux plus vous voir"?' (l.998). It is because he is aware of the implications of this question that Titus now makes a simple statement which, as we have already seen, encapsulates his problem: 'Je viens percer un cœur qui m'adore, qui m'aime' (l.999).

The second group of questions follows immediately (ll.1000-08). Desperately trying to escape from his painful duty, Titus reverts to shorter questions, which, on this occasion, reflect his surprise at what he has been preparing himself to do. His astonishment is emphasized by having two questions and the answer to the second question in a single alexandrine: 'Pourquoi le percer? Qui l'ordonne? Moi-même'. Viewed in this light, Titus's problem seems to vanish. He throws himself, therefore, into a series of single-line questions with an increasingly insistent rhythm which reflects his growing hopes:

Car enfin Rome a-t-elle expliqué ses souhaits?	(4 + 2 + 3 + 3)
L'entendons-nous crier autour de ce palais?	(2 + 4 + 2 + 4)
Vois-je l'état penchant au bord du précipice?	(4 + 2 + 2 + 4)
Ne le puis-je sauver que par ce sacrifice?	(3 + 3 + 3 + 3)

(1001-04)

There follows the statement already quoted concerning Rome's apparent silence before Titus goes on to ask another question in which a new but complementary hope dawns:

Et qui sait si, sensible aux vertus de la reine,
Rome ne voudra point l'avouer pour Romaine?

(1007-08)

Paulin has already told him that there is no chance of this (ll.371-76); but Titus's desire that the impossible should be made to happen blinds him to the truth. One can hear the emotion subverting his reason as he launches himself into a series of rapid monosyllables, reinforced by sliding sibilants ('Et qui *s*ait *s*i, *s*ensible...'), before, picking up the 'r' in 'reine', he triumphantly (but mistakenly) balances 'Rome' and 'Romaine' at either end of the next line.

Some of the questions in the first and second groups are genuine questions: 'Ton cœur te promet-il assez de cruauté?' (l.990); 'Et pourquoi le percer?' (l.1000). All of the questions in the third group are, on the other hand, rhetorical. They reflect Titus's exasperation with himself for so naively succumbing to his own innermost desires. Rome's implacable enmity for everything related to monarchy is expressed in a tellingly short

question occupying one hemistich before being reinforced by a
second question which extends through two-and-a-half lines:

> Quel air respires-tu? N'es-tu pas dans ces lieux
> Où la haine des rois, avec le lait sucée,
> Par crainte ou par amour ne peut être effacée?
>
> (1014-16)

The following cluster of questions builds up to a climax as two
questions of two lines each are immediately followed by a one-
line question. The quickening tempo amply conveys Titus's
exasperation with himself for being so weak:

> Et n'as-tu pas ouï la renommée
> T'annoncer ton devoir jusque dans ton armée?
> Et lorsque Bérénice arriva sur tes pas,
> Ce que Rome en jugeait ne l'entendis-tu pas?
> Faut-il donc tant de fois te le faire redire?
>
> (1019-23)

The fourth group of questions, in which the emperor laments
the time lost since his father's death (ll.1027-36), are also
rhetorical, but they are arranged in a more fluid way. Titus
begins with a two-line question before varying the pattern by
making a statement in the first half of line 1029. This leaves him
with the second hemistich of the same line and the first hemistich
of line 1030 in which to ask a subsequent question, the
deliberately humiliating answer to which is provided in the
remaining hemistich:

> Sont-ce là ces projets de grandeur et de gloire
> Qui devaient dans les cœurs consacrer ma mémoire?
> Depuis huit jours je règne, et, jusques à ce jour,
> Qu'ai-je fait pour l'honneur? J'ai tout fait pour l'amour.
>
> (1027-30)

He then attempts to galvanize himself into action by asking four
one-line questions, which are interrupted by a half-line and a

one-and-a-half line question. The effect of this is to alternately speed up and slow down the rhythm of the actor's delivery as he tries to convey Titus's attempt to whip up the determination he needs if he is to send Bérénice away:

> D'un temps si précieux quel compte puis-je rendre?
> Où sont ces heureux jours que je faisais attendre?
> Quels pleurs ai-je séchés? Dans quels yeux satisfaits
> Ai-je déjà gouté le fruit de mes bienfaits?
> L'univers a-t-il vu changer ses destinées?
> Sais-je combien le ciel m'a compté de journées?
>
> (1031-36)

By distributing Titus's questions in this way, Racine overcomes the rigidity of the four-line module made up of two rhyming couplets which one finds so often in Corneille. Whereas the latter usually makes his sense-units coincide with the end of each alexandrine, Racine is much readier to break the mould at key points. This enables him to throw the more crucial words or ideas into relief ('N'es-tu pas dans ces lieux/Où la haine des rois...', ll.1014-15); and it also helps to create the impression of greater flexibility which one has when reading his verse. The changes of tempo to which I have referred would be much more apparent when one heard the lines being delivered by an experienced actor; but it should not be beyond the scope of the sensitive student to work them out. Here, more than anywhere, it is vital to remember that *Bérénice* is a *play* and that it is meant to be *seen* and *heard* rather than read. Opportunities to see the play are unfortunately very rare, but we can all make the effort to read the lines aloud, or at least to 'listen' to them in our head. Sensitive interpretation is, it should go without saying, essential. Undergraduates who wearily intone (or stumble through) Racine's alexandrines destroy the subtlety of his verse.

The way in which Racine employs imperatives is not as striking as the way in which he distributes Titus's questions; but they, too, reflect the course which the emperor's deliberations are bound to take. Only two imperatives work in Bérénice's favour: Titus's one injunction to Rome ('Que Rome, avec ses lois, mette dans la balance ...', ll.1011-12), and his first injunction to himself: 'Non, non, encore un coup, ne précipitons rien' (l.1010). All the rest militate against her chances of remaining with the man she loves. In lines 1024-25, we have four imperatives in rapid succession:

> Ah! lâche, *fais* l'amour et *renonce* à l'empire.
> Au bout de l'univers *va*, *cours* te confiner,

which are immediately followed by a fifth: '*fais place* à des cœurs plus dignes de régner'. The insistent rhythm, which consistently places the stress on the imperatives (notably the juxtaposed 'va, cours' of line 1025), reveals Titus's disgust at his own weakness. When the same rhythm reappears in the closing lines of his speech, which contain three more imperatives, it reflects his determination to whip up the courage necessary to break his ties with the woman who stands between him and his duty:

> Ne tardons plus, faisons ce que l'honneur exige:
> Rompons le seul lien...
>
> (1039-40)

Racine's frequent use of questions and, to a lesser extent, of imperatives provides a good example of the way in which he utilizes another rhetorical technique: repetition. This is used persuasively both as Titus tries to convince himself that he does not yet need to send Bérénice away ('*Tant de* pleurs, *tant d*'amour, *tant de* persévérance', l.1012) and as he steels himself to accept the truth: 'Depuis huit *jours* je règne, et, jusques à ce *jour*...', l.1029. It is also used to create a leitmotiv effect which, via the different roles which the elements concerned play in the passage, emphasizes the inevitability of the emperor's fate. Thus, Rome, which occurs by name seven times between lines 1001 and 1022, plays no less than three different roles.

When Titus refers to the city in line 1001, he gives it a purely neutral status, asking: 'Car enfin Rome a-t-elle expliqué ses souhaits?' Between line 1007 and 1013, he refers to it on four more occasions, suggesting this time that Rome might actually *favour* the marriage:

> Et qui sait si, sensible aux vertus de la reine,
> *Rome* ne voudra point l'avouer pour Romaine?
> *Rome* peut par son choix justifier le mien.
> Non, non, encore un coup, ne précipitons rien.
> Que *Rome*, avec ses lois, mette dans la balance
> Tant de pleurs, tant d'amour, tant de persévérance.
> *Rome* sera pour nous...

This ecstatic climax soon gives way, as we have seen, to the realization that no such hope can be realistically nurtured. Rome reappears, therefore, with a different role, and in a different stylistic guise. The use of periphrasis emphasizes Titus's new-found understanding of the fact that Rome, *by its very nature*, cannot allow him to marry a queen:

> Quel air respires-tu? N'es-tu pas dans ces lieux
> Où la haine des rois, avec le lait sucée,
> Par crainte ou par amour ne peut être effacée?
>
> (1014-16)

When Rome reappears by name, it is, in consequence, as a stern judge who ruthlessly excludes the luckless Bérénice ('Rome jugea ta reine en condamnant ses rois', l.1017) and condemns Titus for his attempts at evading his duty:

> Et lorsque Bérénice arriva sur tes pas,
> Ce que Rome en jugeait, ne l'entendis-tu pas?
>
> (1021-22)

Rome obviously figures most prominently in the monologue because it reflects Titus's preoccupation with the force which is destroying his happiness. There are, on the other hand, two further examples of repetition, which, though less developed, underline the hopelessness of his fate in exactly the same way. We have seen that it is the prospect of having to face Bérénice's tear-filled eyes that undermines Titus's resolve at the beginning of the passage:

> Quand je verrai ces *yeux* armés de tous leurs charmes,
> Attachés sur les miens, m'accabler de leurs *larmes*,
> Me souviendrai-je alors de mon triste devoir?
>   (995-97)

These are, however, the tears of a single individual. As emperor, Titus feels that it is his duty to dry the tears of *all* his subjects. This moral imperative eventually overrides his distress at hurting Bérénice:

> Quel *pleurs* ai-je séchés? Dans quels *yeux* satisfaits
> Ai-je déjà goûté le fruit de mes bienfaits?
>   (1033-34)

These questions are followed by another in which the full power — and enormous responsibility — of a Roman emperor are laid bare: '*L'univers* a-t-il vu changer ses destinées?' (l.1045). This echoes Titus's earlier chastizement of his cowardice when he disdainfully urged himself to hide in some unknown spot: '*Au bout de l'univers* va, cours te confiner' (l.1025). The ironic echo proves that there is no escape for Titus. The universe is his judge and the symbol of his duty. It cannot provide him with a shameful hiding-place.

The above analysis of the emperor's monologue is far from exhaustive. It has, I hope, shown four things. First, that skilful use of rhetoric can intensify rather than stifle emotion. Second, that Racine can impose order on a highly emotional experience and yet retain the impression of spontaneity. Third, that the playwright succeeds in dramatizing the twists and turns of Titus's mind as he forlornly tries to escape from his duty. Fourth, that, by highlighting the emperor's need to apply as much psychological and emotional pressure on himself as possible, Racine implies that his new-found resolve is neither as rational nor as secure as it might seem on a first reading. This weakness will be exposed in the subsequent confrontation with Bérénice in Act IV scene 5.

4. The Dialogue

The dramatic potential of a dialogue between two characters with very different objectives is much greater than that of a monologue. Racine, however, still has to show how the minds of the emperor and the rejected queen interact, and to portray the conflict between them in a way which is psychologically plausible as well as dramatically exciting. It is my purpose in the present chapter to analyse some of the ways in which he achieved these aims.

Before doing so, I would like to draw the reader's attention to two points of a general nature. The first concerns another of the rules which influenced seventeenth-century tragedy: *les bien-séances*. We have already noted that, for the seventeenth century, tragedy had to be, by definition, an elevated genre. The corollary of this was that, though the protagonists might act in a reprehensible way (Pyrrhus blackmails Andromaque, Hermione orders his death), their behaviour on stage could not depart very far from the standards expected of people of their rank. This is why Titus usually addresses Bérénice as 'Madame' (cf. l.1045), and is normally addressed by her as 'Seigneur' (cf. l.1042). In the same way, both characters refer to each other as 'vous' throughout the play, and reserve 'tu' for their *confidents*.[11] This may seem stilted to a modern reader who is unfamiliar with seventeenth-century tragedy, but it does not impede Racine in the slightest. On the contrary, slight departures from the norm help him to express the characters' deep-seated emotions.[12]

[11] Titus addresses Paulin as 'tu' or 'vous' according to the degree of intimacy he wishes to create (ll.358 ff., 422, 448-49). Bérénice makes Titus address her as 'tu' when criticizing him for not informing her earlier of her fate (ll.1068-70). She does so in order to highlight the affection which the emperor should have shown her and to contrast it with what she regards as his present cruelty. See *12*, pp.28-48.

[12] The switch from 'vous' to 'tu' for a major character shows the full force of passion breaking through social constraints. Good examples may be found in *Andromaque* IV, 5; *Bajazet*, V, 4; *Phèdre*, II, 5.

Thus, when Bérénice apologizes for referring to Titus by his name in front of Paulin (ll.571-72), we can see that it is because her love is welling up inside her. Conversely, when she apostrophizes him as 'cruel' (ll.1062, 1103) or refers to him even more deprecatingly in the third person ('L'ingrat, de mon départ consolé par avance,/Daignera-t-il compter les jours de mon absence?', ll.1119-20), we can appreciate the depth of her anger. The fact that the exchanges between the two protagonists take place within a polite framework which the violence of Bérénice's passion (cf. l.883) is all the time threatening to destroy is, indeed, a positive advantage for Racine since it symbolizes the struggle between violence and control on which this tragedy, like so many others, depends (see below p.83.).

The second point which I want to make at this juncture concerns the nature of the confrontation between Titus and Bérénice. P. France has pointed out, quite rightly, that many of the confrontation scenes in Racine's plays are verbal duels in which the characters fence with each other as they manœuvre for psychological advantage or try to outwit their opponents' schemes (*14*, p.235). *Andromaque* provides several excellent examples: Oreste versus Pyrrhus (I, 2); Pyrrhus versus Andromaque (I, 4); Oreste versus Hermione (II, 2); Hermione versus Pyrrhus (IV, 5). The confrontation between Titus and Bérénice in Act IV scene 5 is superficially very similar: Titus is endeavouring to persuade Bérénice that she must go, while Bérénice is anxious to stay. There is, however, one important difference. Whereas the characters in *Andromaque* can all throw themselves wholeheartedly into the battle, Titus has to hold back. Being only too conscious of the suffering which he is causing Bérénice (ll.990-99) and, from her point of view, of the injustice of what he is doing (ll.502-22), he cannot be as single-minded as he would like. The arguments which he uses to defend himself are not, as we will shortly see, arguments which she can understand; and, worse still, the counter-arguments which she uses against him are all driven home because he has no defence against them. The reason for this is that she is repeating arguments which he had just used when attempting to convince himself in the previous scene that there is no need to send her away. His 'tout se tait' of line 1005 is unknowingly echoed by Bérénice in line 1084, when she asks him why he is sending her away before Rome has taken any action against them: 'Lorsque Rome se tait'. When she goes on to ask him why he is telling her to go now that he is at last the master of his own fate ('Lorsque tout l'univers fléchit à vos genoux,/Enfin quand je n'ai plus à redouter que vous', ll.1085-86), she also echoes his own astonished question and answer in line 1000: 'Et pourquoi le percer? [Bérénice's heart] Qui l'ordonne? Moi-même'. Finally, when she sweeps off threatening suicide, she reminds him of the constancy of her love ('Et sans me repentir de *ma persé-vérance*,/Je me remets sur eux de toute ma vengeance', ll.1195-96) in a way which can only recall his own reasons for believing (momentarily, as we have seen) that Rome might allow her to stay: 'Que Rome, avec ses lois, mette dans la balance/ Tant de pleurs, tant d'amour, *tant de persévérance*./Rome sera pour nous...' (ll.1011-13). The struggle between Titus and Bérénice is, therefore, an unequal battle. The distraught woman can at least lash out and attack the emperor. All he can do is parry her arguments, and he is aware, even then, of the logic behind them. This is why Titus, who has at long last built up enough courage to dismiss Bérénice, loses more and more ground during their confrontation and ends the scene in despair.

The confrontation seems to begin well enough for the emperor. Whereas the advance notice given him of the queen's arrival in Act II had made him weaken (l.554), his determination to go through with his plans has now reached the point where he is unmoved by her unexpected and somewhat vehement entry at line 1040. The fact that *she* is surprised to find him right outside her door ('Ah! Seigneur! vous voici', l.1042) and can confront him only in a subdued and almost submissive way ('il est donc vrai que Titus m'abandonne?/Il faut nous séparer et c'est lui qui l'ordonne?', ll.1043-44) gives him, indeed, a psychological advantage which is reflected in the measured tone of his reply:

N'accablez point, Madame, un prince malheureux,   (4 + 2/2 + 4)
Il ne faut point ici nous attendrir tous deux.   (4 + 2/4 + 2)

The staccato rhythms of Bérénice's words and of Titus's final address to himself in scene 4 have been replaced by rhythms which, though they are not always regular, are firmer and more controlled:

Il en est temps. Forcez votre amour à se taire: (4/1 + 4 + 3)
Et d'un œil que la gloire et la raison éclaire   (3 + 3 + 3 + 3)
Contemplez mon devoir dans toute sa rigueur.   (3 + 3/2 + 4)
                                                                          (1051-53)

Titus's speech thus builds up to a slow, even solemn conclusion as he at last finds the courage necessary to control his emotion (which is still apparent in 'ma princesse') and to confirm Bérénice's worst fears: 'Car enfin, ma princesse, il faut nous séparer' (3 + 3/2 + 4) (l.1061).

The queen, on the other hand, is suddenly consumed by pain and anguish. Picking up Titus's reference to the time it has taken him to find the necessary resolution ('Il en est temps', l.1051), she launches herself into breathless exclamations and despairing questions which are designed to augment his sense of guilt:

Ah! cruel! est-il temps de me le déclarer?   (1 + 2/3 + 4 + 2)
Qu'avez-vous fait? Hélas! je me suis cru aimée.   (4/2/4 + 2)
                                                                          (1062-63)

She then mounts a sustained attack on Titus which, again picking up his words ('Il était temps encor', l.1074), reaches a deliberate crescendo in lines 1081-86, when, having listed all of the obstacles that could have forced them to separate before Vespasian's death (ll.1073-80), she accumulates six subordinate time clauses in five lines as she understandably asks Titus why he has waited so long before sending her away:

Je n'aurais pas, Seigneur, reçu ce coup
Dans le temps que j'espère un bonheur immortel,
Quand votre heureux amour peut tout ce qu'il désire,
Lorsque Rome se tait, *quand* votre père expire,
Lorsque tout l'univers fléchit à vos genoux,
Enfin quand je n'ai plus à redouter que vous.

Bérénice's final statement ignores Titus's appeal to his duty ('Contemplez mon devoir dans toute sa rigueur', l.1053) and puts the responsibility for her dismissal squarely on his shoulders. This is important because it changes the nature of the argument. Whereas Titus had begun by telling Bérénice why she will have to accept the painful situation in which they unexpectedly find themselves, he is now thrown onto the defensive. He has to defend himself, indeed, on two counts. First, why is *he* causing their misfortune? Second, why is he doing so *now*? His answer to the first question casts light on his tragic situation in the play: 'Et c'est moi seul aussi qui pouvais me détruire' (l.1087). He is, in theory, omnipotent; but now feels the weight of responsibility which falls upon his shoulders as emperor. Although no one can force him to do his duty, he himself feels obliged to carry it out (ll.1096-98). As for her second question, he has to accept his guilt in that he loved her so much that he deliberately blinded himself to the realities of his future situation:

Je pouvais vivre alors et me laisser séduire.
Mon cœur se gardait bien d'aller dans l'avenir
Chercher ce qui pouvait un jour nous désunir.

(1088-90)

This is, indeed, one of the tragic flaws in Titus's character which, though it has not created the terrible situation in which he and Bérénice find themselves, is responsible for making that situation much worse than it would otherwise have been. The emperor's honest confession of his guilt in this respect does not, however, undermine his determination to do his duty now: 'Mais il ne s'agit plus de vivre, il faut régner' (l.1102).

In the face of this balanced reassertion of his duty, Bérénice can respond only with insults. Picking up Titus's final words together with an earlier reference to the *gloire* which is forcing him to do his duty (see below p.74), she throws his arguments back in his face, presenting his resigned self-sacrifice as gratuitously cruel self-indulgence: 'Hé bien! régnez, cruel; contentez votre gloire' (l.1103). Trying in desperation to cover up her feelings of rejection and hurt pride, she pretends that she had only come to hear him deny the love which he had sworn to her so often (ll.1104-08).

Reminding him of his earlier declarations of love in the self-same room, she then begins to leave: 'Moi-même j'ai voulu vous entendre en ce lieu./Je n'écoute plus rien, et pour jamais adieu' (ll.1109-10). The words 'Je n'écoute plus rien' seem to indicate that, stung by her misunderstanding of his position, Titus makes as if to reply. But it is not his unspoken words which prevent her from leaving: it is her sudden awareness of the implications of what she has just said. Picking up her own words for once, she falls into a traumatized state as she envisages the empty future which the separated lovers will have to face:

> Pour jamais! Ah! Seigneur, songez-vous en vous-même
> Combien ce mot cruel est affreux quand on aime?
> Dans un mois, dans un an, comment souffrirons-nous,
> Seigneur, que tant de mers me séparent de vous?
> Que le jour recommence et que le jour finisse
> Sans que jamais Titus puisse voir Bérénice,
> Sans que de tout le jour je puisse voir Titus?
>
> (1111-17)

We will have to return to this passage in order to analyse its tragic implications in chapter 5. What we need to note for the moment is the way in which Bérénice suddenly snaps out of her dreamlike state. She has rightly guessed that the separation will be as terrible for Titus as it will be for herself; but, remembering that it is Titus who is sending her away, she leaps to the erroneous conclusion that he does not love her and that he will not suffer at all:

> Mais quelle est mon erreur, et que de soins perdus!
> L'ingrat, de mon départ consolé par avance,
> Daignera-t-il compter les jours de mon absence?
> Ces jours, si longs pour moi, lui sembleront trop courts.
>
> (1118-21)

This bitter attack is even more effective coming as it does after

such spontaneously and intensely expressed emotion. As he tries
to answer it, Titus is being driven even further from his primary
task: convincing Bérénice that it is the political situation in
Rome which is forcing him to send her away. He is reduced
instead to emphasizing the suffering which the separation will
cause *him*. Conscious of the fact that the historical Titus reigned
for only two years, Racine makes his character claim that the
strain of parting from Bérénice will hasten his demise:

> Je n'aurai pas, Madame, à compter tant de jours.
> J'espère que bientôt la triste renommée
> Vous fera confesser que vous étiez aimée.
> Vous verrez que Titus n'a pu, sans expirer...
>
> (1122-25)

This tells us a great deal concerning the strength of the
emperor's new-found determination to do his duty; but Bérénice
though moved by the obvious sincerity of his protestations,
cannot understand his position. If he will suffer to this extent,
then surely some kind of solution must be found. She interrupts
him, therefore, and, swallowing the pride which has just made
her threaten to storm out, she humbles herself by asking if she
may remain in Rome without marrying him (ll.1126-29). This
suggestion has not been considered by Titus, who has no
immediate answer to it. Moved by the queen's heartfelt plea, he
actually succumbs and tells her that she may remain in Rome
(l.1130).

At this point, Titus has lost all the ground he has so painfully
won hitherto. This is an advantage for the dramatist since it
shows that his hero is not a callous brute; but it does not respect
the *données* of the situation which he has set himself the task of
explaining: 'Titus, qui aimait passionnément Bérénice [...], la
renvoya de Rome'. He needs, therefore, to reverse the direction
which the plot is taking whilst at the same time maintaining a
sense of psychological and emotional plausibility. He does this
by making Bérénice react not to *what* Titus is saying (she should
be overjoyed) but to the *way* in which he is saying it. His tone as
he gives in is one of sad lamentation, his lines being slowed down

by a series of marked stresses:

Hélas! vous pouvez tout, Madame. Demeurez: (2/4 + 2 + 4)
Je n'y résiste point. Mais je sens ma faiblesse.   (4 + 2/3 + 3)
                    (1130-31)

The only acceleration comes as he laments the consequences of his decision, picking up the 'sans cesse' of line 1132 and repeating it in the following line:

Il faudra vous combattre et vous craindre sans cesse,
Et sans cesse veiller à retenir mes pas,
Que vers vous à toute heure entraînent vos appas.
                    (1132-34)

The 's' sound, which first appeared in 'je *s*ens ma faible*s*e' is thus repeated six more times ('*s*ans *c*e*ss*e' twice) before becoming a veritable lament in Titus's closing lines:

Que dis-je? En *c*e moment mon cœur, hors de lui-même,
S'oublie, et *s*e *s*ouvient *s*eulement qu'il vous aime.
                    (1135-36)

The emperor's fear here is that, as he loves Bérénice so much, he will find it difficult to tear himself away from her side in order to fulfil the imperial duties for which he has sacrificed their longed-for marriage. Although he does not have the strength to reject Bérénice's compromise solution, he regards it, therefore, as self-defeating. The queen is obviously hurt by his tone, her anger and consternation being underlined by the repetition of 'hé bien!':

Hé bien, Seigneur, hé bien, qu'en peut-il arriver?
Voyez-vous les Romains prêts à se soulever?
                    (1137-38)

This at last gives Titus the chance to return to the theme of duty. Significantly, the political dangers which might spring from the

Romans' hatred of anything to do with kingship are not evoked with reference to Bérénice's desire that he should marry her (he rejects this on purely moral grounds) but with respect to her suggestion that she might merely be allowed to remain in Rome. Titus considers two possible reactions: a revolt which he would have to suppress; or a diminution of his authority as a ruler, which would force him in his turn to compromise with his subjects. His rejection of both possibilities is presented in a series of rhetorical questions (ll.1139-46), to which Bérénice has no rational answer. All she can do is despairingly complain that Titus has not given adequate consideration to her suffering: 'Vous ne comptez pour rien les pleurs de Bérénice' (l.1147). This, we know, is not true since we have seen that, if Titus finds it difficult to go through with his duty, it is not so much because of the suffering which it will cause him as because of the anguish which he is only too aware it will cause the queen. We can sympathize with him, therefore, when, in reply to her understandable but none the less unjust reproach, he exclaims: 'Je les compte pour rien! Ah! ciel! quelle injustice!' (l.1148).

Seeing him weaken, Bérénice drives home her advantage by asking him why he is destroying his happiness, suggesting as she does so that he should try to strike a balance between the rights of Rome and his own rights as an individual: 'Rome a ses droits, Seigneur: n'avez-vous pas les vôtres?' (ll.1156-68). His inability to reply is underlined by the queen's injunctions: 'Dites, parlez' (l.1153). When he does manage to force some words out, he can only lament: 'Hélas! que vous me déchirez!' (ibid). Titus seems, at this point, to be at an all-time low. Unable to answer Bérénice's questions adequately, he is reduced, as the queen is quick to notice, to tears: 'Vous êtes empereur, Seigneur, et vous pleurez!' (l.1154).

This statement may be a reference to Marie Mancini's comment to the young Louis XIV when they parted (*4*, p.89 n.2); but Racine would not have included it merely for that reason. Its function here is to echo a literary commonplace (the unhappiness of the mighty — cf. *Iphigénie* I, 1), and, more importantly still, to act as a spur to Titus. Bérénice is so in love with him that she naturally assumes that, if he is sending her away, it is because he no longer loves her. She is totally taken aback, therefore, at the spectacle of the grief which would not be experienced by an unfeeling ex-lover. As she comments on it, she unwittingly gives Titus the opportunity he needs to return to the attack. Although he cannot bear to see the sufferings of the woman he loves, he *is* able to face up to his own anguish. When he picks up her words ('Oui, Madame, il est vrai, je pleure, je soupire,/Je frémis'), it is not, therefore, as a taunt. It is as a concession before he launches himself into a tirade which contrasts with his broken speech of seconds before. Citing the examples of various Romans who have sacrificed personal feelings for the greater good of Rome, he claims that the sacrifice which he is making surpasses theirs, and asks Bérénice, by way of a conclusion, whether she believes that he is incapable of living up to Rome's high standards (ll.1155-74).

Titus's preoccupation with heroics, and with other people's opinion of him, will need discussion in the next chapter. It is more important to note for the moment that, having wavered in the face of Bérénice's onslaught, Titus has now regained the ground he had lost and is affirming once again his determination to obey the laws of Rome: 'Il les faut maintenir' (l.1158). This is more than the queen can take. Thus, the scene moves to its climax as she once again picks up the emperor's words ('me croyez-vous *indigne*/De laisser un exemple à la postérité/Qui *sans de grands efforts* ne puisse être imité?') and throws them back in his face: 'Non, je crois tout *facile* à votre barbarie./Je vous crois *digne*, ingrat, de m'arracher la vie' (ll.1172-76). Now that her love stands no chance of being fulfilled, her pride returns. It is reflected both in her rejection of her own suggestion that she remain in Rome without marrying Titus and in her pretence that she wanted to force him to send her away:

> Qui, moi? j'aurais voulu, honteuse et méprisée,
> D'un peuple qui me hait soutenir la risée?
> J'ai voulu vous pousser jusques à ce refus.
>
> (1179-81)

Her love is, however, too great to be so simply repressed. If she is unable to fulfil it, there is, as she now makes clear to Titus, only one solution: suicide. Something tells her, deep down, that, despite his apparently uncaring behaviour, he does still love her, but she uses that knowledge only in order to accentuate his sense of guilt at having driven her to take her life:

> Si devant que mourir la triste Bérénice
> Vous veut de son trépas laisser quelque vengeur,
> Je ne le cherche, ingrat, qu'au fond de votre cœur.
> Je sais que tant d'amour n'en peut être effacée [...]
> (1188-91)

The confrontation between the two characters is thus brought to a natural conclusion as, like Titus in Act II, Bérénice rushes from the stage.

My analysis of this scene is, once again, far from exhaustive. It has been analysed in enough detail for us to see, however, that Racine makes it dramatic by concentrating on the interaction of two fundamentally unstable characters. Titus begins the scene firmly enough, but wavers in the face of Bérénice's onslaught. Although he finds enough determination to regain the ground he has lost, he is plunged into even deeper despair by the queen's threat to commit suicide. Bérénice, for her part, is at first subdued, then angry, beseeching, surprised and furious once more. The tempo of the scene varies in consequence. It begins abruptly with Bérénice's unexpected entry, but then slows down as she fearfully asks the question on which her future depends and Titus gives his deliberately measured reply. The pace quickens as Bérénice becomes more and more incensed; but slows right down as Titus unwillingly gives in to the queen's pleas; and almost grinds to a halt as, unable to answer her subsequent challenge, the emperor is reduced to tears. There is then a dramatic contrast as he suddenly regains his determination to do his duty and Bérénice's pleading is replaced by threats inspired by white-hot anger.

These changes of tempo may be hard to pick up when one is reading the text. The reader should note, however, that they are an essential part of good drama: the rhythm with which a play

unfolds will be different from that with which our eyes normally
scan a text. He should note further that it would be a mistake to
assume that a play must contain 'action' if it is to be dramatic.
Hugo's plays are far more eventful than *Bérénice*; but I doubt
whether they contain anything more dramatic than Racine's
skilful manipulation of the changing relations between Bérénice
and Titus. The spectacle of two people who, though deeply in
love, are tearing each other apart because of a misunderstanding
(Bérénice is in despair because she feels that Titus is unmoved by
her sufferings; Titus is racked by anguish because he *is* moved by
them) is nothing short of spell-binding. It also proves that
Voltaire was wrong to regard *Bérénice* as a 'tragédie à l'eau rose'
(quoted in *4*, p.133).

5. Tragedy

Although admitting that *Bérénice* drew tears from its audience, Voltaire felt that its subject was not sufficiently tragic: 'Un amant et une maîtresse qui se quittent ne sont pas sans doute un sujet de tragédie' (quoted in *4*, p.114). Racine had foreseen his objection and tried to counter it in his preface, where he argues that the separation of Titus and Bérénice is on a par with the celebrated story of Aeneas and Dido. The Carthaginian queen killed herself when Aeneas abandoned her, but a play can be tragic, Racine argues, without blood and death:

> Ce n'est point une nécessité qu'il y ait du sang et des morts dans une tragédie; il suffit que l'action en soit grande, que les acteurs en soient héroïques, que les passions y soient excitées, et que tout s'y ressente de cette tristesse majestueuse qui fait tout le plaisir de la tragédie. (p.27)

There is no doubt that, technically, Racine was right. To qualify as a tragedy, in seventeenth-century terms, a play had only to involve noble characters one or more of whom was exposed to a threat of death[13] — as Bérénice, Titus and Antiochus all are since they contemplate suicide. In referring to 'cette tristesse majestueuse qui fait tout le plaisir de la tragédie', the playwright seems, however, to be going beyond technical definitions in order to claim that his play makes the emotional impact which we associate with tragedies.[14] This, therefore, is the question to

[13] See R.C. Knight, 'A minimal definition of seventeenth-century tragedy', *French Studies*, 10 (1956), pp.297-308.

[14] Wishing to defend *Bérénice*, Racine writes as if all tragedies created the same emotional response. This is clearly not true. Cf. the prefaces to *Iphigénie* and *Phèdre*, in which Racine refers to the creation of compassion (which is more intense than 'tristesse'?) and terror (which *Bérénice* does not seem to inspire). Rightly emphasizing the 'variety of [his] characterization and the breadth of his vision', Yarrow argues that Racine's plays cannot be made to fit a single tragic pattern (*33*, chapter 6). For a stimulating attempt to interpret Racine in the light

which we must address ourselves in the following pages.

That *Bérénice* creates sadness in its readers and spectators seems to be fairly obvious, particularly in so far as its protagonists are all victims of situations over which they have little or no control. Thus, Antiochus is, as he rightly claims, 'D'un inutile amour [la] trop constante victime' (l.255). He fell in love with Bérénice before she had met Titus and was regarded as an acceptable suitor until challenged by a rival whose immediate success sounded the death-knell of his hopes: 'Titus, pour mon malheur, vint, vous vit et vous plut' (l.194). Although rebuffed by Bérénice and made to swear never to speak of his love again (ll.199-205), Antiochus found himself following her to Italy, where his sufferings became even more intense when Titus and Bérénice both confided their love for each other to him (ll.240-44, 1435-36). He was unable to tear himself away, however, and remained in Rome in the hope that, while Vespasian ruled, some obstacle would prevent the future emperor from marrying his chosen bride (ll.245-48). This obstacle materializes from an unexpected quarter (Titus himself); but Antiochus's role as passive victim continues during the play. His hopes are successively raised (III, 2; V, 2) only to be immediately and cruelly dashed. The ups and downs of his fate exacerbate his already intense suffering and, rather than witness (as he thinks) the apotheosis of a requited love from which he is excluded, he resolves to commit suicide (ll.1293-1302). An even worse shock awaits him when he learns that, even though Titus and Bérénice are not to be married, the queen cannot love him. Significantly, it is Bérénice who imposes his future course of conduct: he must follow her example and remain alive even though he longs for death (ll.1495-1502).

Antiochus is particularly worthy of our sympathy because, unlike the other frustrated lovers in Racine's plays, he is moved by the suffering of the unattainable object of his desire. Whereas Hermione and Roxane order the destruction of the men who spurn them, Antiochus can pity Bérénice even when she has just treated him most unfairly. This is why he delays his departure

of the traditional Aristotelian schema of hubris, error and ultimate enlightenment, see 9, chapter 8 (pp.244-46 are devoted to *Bérénice*).

from Rome at the end of Act III (ll.944-52). At the end of Act IV, he shows even more self-abnegation when he pleads with Titus to return to the suicidal queen (ll.1227-39). Many unsuccessful suitors would be tempted to blacken the image of their rivals, but Antiochus loves Bérénice too much to do so, insisting instead on the distress which the enforced separation is causing Titus (ll.896-902, 936-40). The pity which he inspires in us can only be increased still further, therefore, when we see him being so cruelly treated both by Bérénice and by the emperor. The latter is less blameworthy in this respect since he is ignorant of the love which his rival has kept secret; but he is insensitive, to say the least, to the suffering which is causing his friend to leave Rome so suddenly (ll.667-84). He must bear some of the responsibility, therefore, for the pain which he inflicts on Antiochus when he asks him to act as a go-between. Bérénice, for her part, is fully aware of Antiochus's undying love for her, but treats him in a haughty, unfeeling manner (ll.259-62), and accuses him of lying even when she is half-conscious of the fact that he must be telling the truth (ll.914-18).

When the play is studied in this light, one can begin to understand why Villars argues that Antiochus is the only sympathetic character in the play (see *41*, p.251). He is, however, oversimplifying the situation since the unfair treatment handed out to Antiochus by Titus and Bérénice is the result of the fact that they too are victims. The difference is that, in their case, the emotional problems which they experience are created by political constraints.

The suffering caused by these constraints appears even more tragic when one realizes that they have little or no rational basis. Since it was Bérénice who helped inspire Titus with his love of virtue (ll.502-18), it is unjust that his desire to do his duty should rebound so tragically on her (ll.519-22). The injustice is made more flagrant still by the fact that, whereas Bérénice is known to have the moral potential associated with the highest Roman standards, she is unable to become Titus's consort simply because she is a queen (ll.375-76). Yet, as the emperor himself laments (ll.727-30), he would be perfectly free to marry any Roman woman, however unworthy she might otherwise be.

Even Paulin is unable to justify the prejudice against Bérénice on rational grounds. He admits that the title of king ('ce nom si noble et si saint autrefois', l.382) is not intrinsically evil; and, when informing Titus of the Roman people's enmity towards the woman he loves, prefaces his remarks with the telling concession: 'soit raison, *soit caprice,*/Rome ne l'attend point pour son impératrice' (ll.382, 371-72). The prejudice in question might be more acceptable if it were a sincere reflection of the Romans' traditionally very passionate commitment to freedom. But it is not. It is a mere remnant of their past traditions, an empty shell to which they blindly cling even though their liberty has long since been destroyed by the imperial regime (ll.385-86). One wonders whether Titus is right, therefore, when, rejecting the judgment of his sycophantic courtiers, he proclaims his desire to live up to the standards of the allegedly nobler Roman people (ll.351-56). His later rejection of Bérénice's desire to flee from a city in which she is mocked by the populace ('Ecoutez-vous, Madame, une foule insensée?', l.1319) seems to provide a more accurate assessment of the true value of the subservient Roman people.

It would seem, in consequence, that Bérénice is right when she suggests that Titus should change the 'injustes lois' which are destroying their happiness (ll.1149-50). Titus certainly intended to change them before he became emperor (ll.435-38); but now, at the very moment when he believed that he would be free to give expression to his love (l.713), he has discovered that his new-found moral integrity will simply not allow him to do so. We have seen that the emperor attributes his conversion from a pleasure-seeking courtier in the retinue of Nero to a man with high moral standards to the influence of Bérénice; but this 'conversion' can only have been partial. This is proved not only by his firm intention (at that time) to break his country's most fundamental (if irrational) law but also by his wish that his father might die so that he could make Bérénice empress (ll.431-38). His supposed 'virtue' was, at this stage, little more than a superior way of expressing his love:

Bérénice me plut. Que ne fait point un cœur
Pour plaire à ce qu'il aime et gagner son vainqueur?
Je prodiguai mon sang; tout fit place à mes armes.
Je revins triomphant. Mais le sang et les larmes
Ne me suffisaient pas pour mériter ses vœux:
J'entrepris le bonheur de mille malheureux.

(509-14)

While ostensibly fulfilling the desires of others, he was really indulging both himself and Bérénice (who approved of his 'virtuous' activities): 'Heureux, et plus heureux que tu ne peux comprendre,/Quand je pouvais paraître à ses yeux satisfaits/Chargés de mille cœurs conquis par mes bienfaits (ll.516-18). The cruel lesson which Titus has to learn is that virtue is not an idyllic charade, that it involves self-sacrifice as well as self-gratification. This lesson was not driven home until he actually became emperor, the momentous nature of the experience being stressed by the fact that he describes it twice, firstly to Paulin and secondly to Bérénice herself:

Mais à peine le ciel eut rappelé mon père,
Dès que ma triste main eut fermé sa paupière,
De mon aimable erreur je fus désabusé:
Je sentis le fardeau qui m'était imposé;
Je connus que bientôt, loin d'être à ce que j'aime,
Il fallait, cher Paulin, renoncer à moi-même.

(459-64)

Tout l'empire parlait. Mais la gloire, Madame,
Ne s'était point encor fait entendre à mon cœur
Du ton dont elle parle au cœur d'un Empereur.
Je sais tous les tourments où ce dessein me livre.
Je sais bien que sans vous je ne saurais plus vivre,
Que mon cœur de moi-même est prêt à s'éloigner;
Mais il ne s'agit plus de vivre, il faut régner.

(1096-1102)

The tragic consequences of this moment of recognition are

(admittedly in a very different way) every bit as moving as the results of the excruciating revelation vouchsafed, equally tardily, to Oedipus. Titus, whose life revolves around Bérénice, will be obliged to live in emotional exile without her (ll.751-54). Although forced to remain alive in order to do his duty, his only hope is that fate will take pity on him and end his living death (ll.755-56, 1100, 1122-25). During the course of the play, he is also constrained to witness the suffering he is inflicting on Bérénice and to suffer, in his turn, from the bitter criticisms of the woman who is convinced that he has betrayed her love. It is little wonder that, tortured by her incomprehension of his newly-discovered position, he ends up threatening to commit suicide before her eyes (ll.1420-22).

Approached in this way, Titus can be seen to be in an even more tragic situation than Antiochus. I know from experience, however, that undergraduates may well nurture doubts about Titus's motivation which would substantially reduce their assessment of his tragic stature. First, does he really love Bérénice? Second, does he comply with Roman pressure out of a sense of fear rather than as a result of moral conviction? Third, does his reference to his *gloire* imply, as we have seen Bérénice suggest, that he is egotistically sacrificing one passion in order to fulfil another which is dearer to his heart?

The first question has been answered in the negative by no less a critic than Roland Barthes, who argues: 'C'est Bérénice qui désire Titus. Titus n'est lié à Bérénice que par l'habitude' (*10*, p.94). The reader cannot be warned too strongly, however, against basing his or her interpretations of Racine on *a priori* assumptions which do not accord with the text. Antiochus does suggest on one occasion that Titus's protestations of love for Bérénice might be exaggerated (ll.939-40), but this is when he is under stress because of the queen's unfair treatment of him. Titus, as we have seen (p.23), reaffirms the depth of his love in circumstances in which he has no reason to lie. Although he has loved the queen for five years, his desire to see her is still as fresh as it was when they first met: 'Depuis cinq ans entiers chaque jour je la vois,/Et crois toujours la voir pour la première fois' (ll.545-46). Her love for him is so intense that some men

(Constant's Adolphe, for example) might find it overpowering; but there is no sign of irritation in Titus's voice as he describes the passion which makes her wish to see him whenever possible (ll.534-40). On the contrary, he feels exactly the same overwhelming need to see her. This is why he is so unhappy about allowing her to remain in Rome without marrying him (see above p.62).

Doubts about the sincerity of Titus's references to the overwhelming demands of his duty have been expressed by another modern critic: Jean Prophète, who sees fear rather than patriotic duty as the main motive for the emperor's decision to reject the queen: 'Il n'a pas le sens du devoir, il n'en a que les frayeurs. Il ne craint pas le "qu'en dira-t-on"; il a peur du "qu'en fera-t-on" ' (*28*, pp.58-59). This judgment recognizes the constraints from which Titus is suffering more than Barthes is prepared to (he sees them merely as a convenient alibi); but it, too, is based on a temptation to which students of Racine should be careful not to succumb: arbitrary distortion of the text. We have seen (above, p.16) that Titus is only too aware of the pressure which Rome is exerting on him, and that, at most junctures in the play, he takes this pressure very seriously. There is no need, on the other hand, to regard justified concern as ignoble fear. Part of Titus's problem in convincing Bérénice that Roman traditions are such that he really must send her away is, as we noted earlier (p.15), that he wishes to make his own decision *before* the Romans have tried to enforce, or even publically expressed, their opinion. We have seen, too, that, though Titus is well aware that the Romans will disapprove of any attempt on his part to avoid sending her away, he does not assume that they will necessarily revolt. Even if they were to rebel against him, he shows no sign of fearing defeat. His only concern is that he would be forced to spill his *citizens'* blood (ll.1140-41). He is certainly afraid that a rebellious mob might humiliate Bérénice (ll.732-34), but he shows no fear on his own account at all. As a brave soldier (ll.218-24) with no obvious military or dynastic problems, there is no reason why he should. Given the fact that he looks forward to death as a solution to his dilemma, it is more than likely that, if there were any military dangers, he would welcome the chance to die in battle rather than see the departure of the woman he loves (see lines 499-501, 1093-94, also *36*).

The third question which might be raised about the emperor's motivation (is he achieving some kind of fulfilment through the pursuit of glory?) is much trickier because he has a passion for fame which he describes in similar terms to his love for Bérénice (ll.1134, 502-03). It is also his *gloire* that he invokes when informing Bérénice of the moral transformation that he experienced when he succeeded his father: 'Mais la gloire, Madame,/Ne s'était point encor fait entendre à mon cœur/Du ton dont elle parle au cœur d'un empereur' (ll.1096-98). Bérénice interprets this as proof of the egotism which has, she feels, replaced his love for her (l.1103); but care is needed since *gloire* in the seventeenth century could refer either to one's reputation in the eyes of other people or to one's own assessment of one's merits (see *4*, p.23). Titus is influenced by both concepts. On the one hand, the anguish which the separation from Bérénice is causing him is such that he needs to use the idea of his reputation in the eyes of others as a crutch with which to support his wavering resolution (see below, p.80). On the other, he is gripped by an inwardly apprehended moral imperative which, although it is forcing him to comply with the most senseless of Roman traditions, allows him no escape. Hence the self-laceration in which we have seen him indulge in his monologue in Act IV (above, p.52). Hence, too, the uncompromising statement to Bérénice as he presents her with his ultimatum in Act V:

Ma gloire inexorable à toute heure me suit;
Sans cesse elle présente à mon âme étonnée
L'empire incompatible avec votre hyménée.

(1394-96)

She has turned him into an emperor who develops higher moral standards than either he or she had suspected; but he cannot abandon them without denying everything that their love has come to symbolize. This is why Titus is right when he tells her that she would despise him as much as he would despise himself if he took the coward's way out and abdicated (ll.1403-06). It is for the same reason that Titus and Bérénice must ultimately agree to part rather than wait to see if they will have to respond to the catcalls of the Roman mob. We have seen that the incredulous question which brought Titus hope in Act IV ('Qui l'ordonne? Moi-même', l.1000) is replaced by the despairing admission of helplessness in the ensuing confrontation with the queen: 'Et c'est moi seul aussi qui pouvais me détruire' (l.1087). We can see now that this admission epitomizes Titus's plight. Love for Bérénice and the experience of becoming emperor have endowed him with a moral integrity such that he cannot back away from his duty. He tries to do so on no less than three occasions (IV, 4; IV, 5; V, 5); but he is eventually forced to recognize that he was right when he stated earlier in the play that he must force himself to do his duty however much personal suffering it may cause him: 'Je connais mon devoir, c'est à moi de le suivre:/Je n'examine point si j'y pourrai survivre' (ll.551-52).

If it is hard for Titus to reach a proper understanding of the situation in which he unexpectedly finds himself, it is obviously much harder for Bérénice, as a foreigner, to understand the need for her departure. She wonders, quite understandably, what it is that she has done to deserve the animosity which makes the Roman people rejoice at the news of her decision to leave the city, and wins our sympathy as she asks, in total bewilderment, if loving Titus can be a crime: 'Quel crime, quelle offense a pu les animer?/Hélas! et qu'ai-je fait que de vous trop aimer?' (ll.1317-18). The Roman prejudices from which she suffers can only seem to her to be an example of gratuitous cruelty which has wrought an incomprehensible change in the man she loves. Hence her rebuke to him in Act V: 'Retournez, retournez vers ce sénat auguste/Qui vient vous applaudir de votre cruauté' (ll.1328-29).

Her confusion and devastation are made worse by the fact that, though her relationship with him had always been opposed by the Romans, Titus had continually reassured her that she was in no danger: 'il a cent fois/Rassuré mon amour contre leurs dures lois,/Cent fois...' (ll.641-43). These reassurances were reinforced, moreover, by numerous promises of marriage, which are now, apparently inexplicably, being broken: 'Après tant de serments, Titus m'abandonner!/Titus qui me jurait... Non, je ne le puis croire ...' (ll.906-07). Worse still, these promises are being broken not at a time when she knew that their relationship was under threat but at a time when Titus is at long last in a position, as she believes, to keep his word and marry her. Because of his belated change of mind, she is now in the terrible position of seeing her happiness elude her just at the moment when she believes that it is within her grasp: 'Dans le temps que j'espère un bonheur immortel', as she aggrievedly puts it (l.1082).

Bérénice makes her problems worse as a result of her refusal to heed Phénice's warning at the end of Act I, and, more obviously still, as a result of her almost wilfully blind desire to misinterpret the emperor's strange behaviour in Act II (see above, p.26). There are, however, extenuating circumstances, notably Titus's understandable but none the less cruel evasion of his duty to inform her clearly of the change in her situation. He says enough in their first confrontation to make the queen react in an anxious, irrational way, but not enough to leave her in no doubt about the nature of the problem. As a woman whose whole being is totally absorbed in that of the man she loves (ll.1064-65), she is afraid that she loves him so much that he may stop loving her (ll.632-34). It is natural, therefore, that she should assume that this fear has been cruelly fulfilled (ll.620, 664, 977-78, 1480-81), and express blank incomprehension when the man who is sending her away after so many promises of marriage insists that he still loves her: 'Vous m'aimez, vous me le soutenez,/Et cependant je pars, et vous me l'ordonnez?' (ll.1345-46). Although haughty with Antiochus (ll.259-62), she does not have the deep-seated pride which would enable her to pretend like Hermione that hatred can take the place of betrayed passion (cf. *Andromaque*, II, 1). All she can do is insist that her love for Titus is such an integral part of her existence that, without his love for her, she will die (ll.615-16, 645-46, 975-76, 1176, 1185-93). Antiochus's vivid description of her demented state at the end of Act IV makes it clear that her suicide threat, which is the logical consequence of her total commitment to Titus, is no empty charade:

> Qu'avez-vous fait, Seigneur? l'aimable Bérénice
> Va peut-être expirer dans les bras de Phénice.
> Elle n'entend ni pleurs, ni conseils, ni raison;
> Elle implore à grands cris le fer et le poison.
>
> (1227-30)

Nor is it a threat which, made in the heat of the moment, will be quickly abandoned later. She remains suicidal, as we have seen, after she has had a chance to recover from the immediate shock created by Titus's confirmation of his decision to do his duty.

In the event, Bérénice is subsequently persuaded not to commit suicide by Titus's own threat to kill himself if she does. When she agrees to live, his threat has no reason to be fulfilled. The Abbé de Villars made much of this when attempting to satirize the play: 'l'effet de l'amour le plus ordinaire, et le plus vraisemblable, c'est de se tuer soi-même, ou du moins de faillir à le faire, comme on le voit en Titus, Bérénice et Antiochus' (see *41*, p.249). Villars's argument must have annoyed Racine intensely since it was precisely his intention to try to prove in *Bérénice* that staying alive can be more tragic than committing suicide. Antiochus has to live with the knowledge that, even when separated from Titus, Bérénice cannot find room in her heart for him (ll.1447-49). The emperor has to turn his back on everything which gives his personal existence its meaning ('Il ne s'agit plus de vivre, il faut régner', l.1102). As for Bérénice, she will find herself in the permanent nightmare so graphically evoked in her argument with Titus in Act IV, where, bidding him an angry goodbye, she is suddenly paralysed by the awful awareness of what eternal separation really means:

> Je n'écoute plus rien, et pour jamais adieu.
> Pour jamais! Ah! Seigneur, songez-vous en vous-même
> Combien ce mot cruel est affreux quand on aime?
> Dans un mois, dans un an, comment souffrirons-nous,

> Seigneur, que tant de mers me séparent de vous?
> Que le jour recommence et que le jour finisse
> Sans que jamais Titus puisse voir Bérénice,
> Sans que de tout le jour je puisse voir Titus?
>
>   (1110-17)

The two lovers will be separated geographically by 'tant de mers', but it is the unending nature of the separation which frightens Bérénice. For a woman who suffers anguish when separated from Titus even for a moment (ll.613-14), the prospect of months and years of separation is terrifying. As she pursues her nightmarish perspective, however, the emptiness of a life without Titus is not evoked through longer chronological units but by individual days:

> Que *le jour* recommence et que *le jour* finisse
> Sans que jamais Titus puisse voir Bérénice,
> Sans que *de tout le jour* je puisse voir Titus?

Even here, the perspective narrows still further since the queen begins by evoking successive days which are conveyed by the prefix of the verb '*re*commencer', through the 'commencer'/ 'finir' cycle and through the repetition of 'jour' in stressed positions in the same line (l.1115). In the last line quoted, on the other hand, Bérénice envisages the anguish of having to live through *each* empty day without being able to see the man that she loves. Her desperation is amplified by the inversion of the verb and its adverbial complement, as well as by the fact that both 'tout' and 'jour' are stressed.

This section of the queen's speech is an integral part of her address to the emperor; but it is emotionally and poetically so intense that it also stands out from its immediate context and becomes a lyrical lament evoking the lovers' future fate. The frequent repetitions ('*Dans un* mois, *dans un* an'; '*Que le jour* recommence et *que le jour* finisse', 'de tout *le jour*'; '*Sans que* jamais Titus *puisse voir* Bérénice,/*Sans que* [...] je *puisse voir* Titus') combine with insistent assonances /'*Dans un m*ois, d*ans un an, comment* souff*rirons-n*ous,/Seigneu*r*'; 'Que le jou*r* finisse/Sans que jamais Titus puisse voir Bérénice/Sans que de tout le jour je puisse voir Titus') to create an incantatory effect which engraves these lines on the memory of the reader/ spectator, who will remember them, and their implications, at the end of the play when Bérénice exits from the stage, leaving Titus as exiled as herself (ll.751-56) and sending Antiochus back alone to his empty kingdom (l.234).

It should be obvious from the above that *Bérénice* will create sadness in anyone who is prepared to identify reasonably closely with Racine's protagonists. It must be confessed, however, that we have seen very little which would seem to justify his claim that the play creates an atmosphere of *majestic* sadness. Titus, as Villars was quick to point out (see *41*, pp.249-50), is in an invidious position because, whatever his duties to Rome, he is breaking his promises to Bérénice. Hence the queen's own accusation:

Après tant de serments, Titus m'abandonner!
Titus qui me jurait...Non, je ne le puis croire:
Il ne me quitte point, il y va de sa gloire.

(906-08)

We have no reason to doubt that he proved to be a brave soldier in the war against the Jews (ll.218-24); but his role in the play (which is bound to affect us more strongly) is weak and vacillating. The empathy which makes him worry so much about making Bérénice suffer is an attractive trait, but his attempt to avoid explaining matters to her properly is surely an act of moral cowardice. He manages to overcome this and to face Bérénice himself in Act IV; but, though he begins the scene with dignity, he soon weakens to the point where he is reduced to tears by the queen's arguments and to despair by her suicide threat. He does, it is true, regain the lost ground in Act V and present the queen with an ultimatum which forces her to accept the situation. According to Bettina Knapp (*19*, p.112), this is the moment when he matures from a dependent adolescent into a mature adult; but the weaknesses are still there. To begin with, he is clearly reacting to the *emotional* shock of discovering the true purport of Bérénice's letter, and is swinging wildly from one course of action (telling Bérénice to stay, line 1312) to another: telling her to go (line 1391 ff.). Although he likes to think that his suicide threat puts him in the same mould as the great Roman heroes of the past (ll.1408-14), it is really an act of despair which Villars is quite right to identify with emotional weakness (see *41*, p.249). Although Knapp presents Titus as a 'hero who sees his course with lucidity, who knows what his way must be', she is forced to recognize (*19*, pp.112, 118) that, even at the moment when the emperor is supposed to be most clearly aware of his own moral identity, he still needs to lean on Bérénice by making his course of action dependent on hers ('Vous voilà de mes jours maintenant responsable', l.1424). Even though his decision to reject the queen is inspired by his own inwardly apprehended sense of duty (see above, p.71, 74), he needs, too, to lean on other people's view of him. This is why he appeals both to Bérénice and to the world in his ultimatum speech:

> *Vous-même rougiriez de ma lâche conduite*:
> Vous verriez à regret marcher à votre suite
> Un indigne empereur sans empire, sans cour,
> *Vil spectacle aux humains* des faiblesses d'amour.
>
> (1403-06)

It is for the same reason that he keeps appealing to the unfortunate Antiochus to come and witness his suffering (ll.1291-92, 1426-29). Titus was brought up as a passive creature idly following the bad example set by Nero's court (ll.506-08). His partial transformation at the hands of Bérénice was equally passive (ll.502-03), and, even when he is at his strongest in the play, he still feels the need to ask her for her support (ll.1055-56). In his moment of utter despair in Act V, Titus sees clearly that he cannot escape from his duty, but he cannot find the calm self-control of the Roman heroes with whom he is continually trying to identify (ll.1158-74). As he himself confesses to Bérénice: 'Je croyais ma vertu [moral courage] moins prête à succomber,/Et j'ai honte du trouble où je la vois tomber' (ll.1373-74). Titus's sufferings certainly make him sympathetic, but they can hardly be said to make him very dignified, and still less majestic.

We are told towards the beginning of the play that Bérénice has the Roman virtues which Titus would so dearly like to possess (ll.375-76). It must be said, however, that, prior to Act V scene 7, these virtues are not in evidence. Although Phénice tells her that she will have to show all her courage in the face of Titus's decision to send her away ('Il faut ici montrer la grandeur de votre âme', l.904), she gives way instead to a combination of self-pity and despair which expresses itself in an urge to lash out and hurt the man she loves. This blind rage is easily explicable in view of the five years of love and promises of marriage which Titus is betraying; but it puts Bérénice in an awkward posture. Whereas she accuses him of having no regard for her feelings, Titus and the audience know full well that this is not true (ll.1147-48). Even Phénice rebukes her for her unfair attitude towards the emperor, whose tears she had described to her mistress (ll.965, 979). It is, on the other hand, the queen's attitude to Antiochus which most clearly highlights the self-centredness of her passion. Apparently forgetting his earlier declaration of love (ll.199-208), she reacts with shock and anger to his confession in Act I, and is so obsessed with Titus that she is prepared to consign her erstwhile friend and *confident* to prompt oblivion if he threatens, however remotely, to come between her and the man she hopes to marry (ll.259 ff., 289-91). She is even more unfair to him in Act III, when she cruelly appeals to his love for her (l.878) in order to blackmail him into delivering Titus's message, and then accuses him of lying (ll.914-15). Antiochus rightly resents his fate: 'Avec quelle injustice et quelle indignité/Elle doute à mes yeux de ma sincérité!' (ll.933-34).

At this point in the play, Bérénice has, indeed, begun to lose her dignity. She jeopardizes it still further (as she later realizes, ll.1179-80) by offering to remain in Rome without marrying Titus. She is also happy to let the emperor see her in her dishevelled state (ll.972-78), and enters and exits in Act IV in a most undignified way. She does not behave with any more decorum in Act V, where she rushes on to the stage in order to flee from Titus, and then finds her path blocked when she attempts to escape from his presence (ll.1357-58). Some undergraduates resent the use of suddenly discovered letters in otherwise tightly constructed tragedies (cf. *Bajazet* IV, 5); but the way in which Titus snatches Bérénice's letter from her hands in Act V scene 5 epitomizes the undignified position to which both protagonists have allowed themselves to sink. *Bérénice* is a play about recognition of the truth: Titus has to recognize that there is no escape from his duty; and Bérénice has to be brought to the point where she can understand that the emperor does love her and that he is motivated by political constraints. The queen can only undermine her tragic stature, therefore, when she has recourse to a subterfuge in order to escape from Rome. Titus's moral stature is diminished, too, when, having discovered the truth about Bérénice's ploy, he abandons all attempts at rational persuasion and resorts instead to the crudest form of moral blackmail: do as I say, or I will kill myself.

It looks, therefore, as if Villars was right in arguing that Titus and Bérénice are too undignified to be tragic (see *41*, p. 247-51). Surprising as it may seem, this was what Racine, in large measure, probably wanted him (and us) to think. The difference, however, is that Racine was playing a game of brinkmanship in which the tragic stature of the emperor and the queen was to be unexpectedly rescued at the last minute.[15] Both of the main protagonists contribute to this sudden reversal of their situation, but in unequal measure.

When Titus moves from abject pleading with the queen to bold defiance ('Ne vous attendez point que, las de tant d'alarmes,/Par un heureux hymen je tarisse vos larmes', ll.1391-92), he begins the process; but his resolve still contains the serious flaws which I have already discussed. The main source of tragic dignity at the end of the play is Bérénice (this is why the play is named after her). Antoine Adam has suggested, somewhat deprecatingly, that, as a mere woman, the queen cannot

[15] If I am right, this would explain why Racine is so obviously stung by Villars's criticisms (see his preface, pp.29-30). Louis Racine tells us that he was even more upset by Chapelle's comment on his heroine: 'Marion pleure, Marion crie, Marion veut qu'on la marie' (*41*, p.63). This insensitive jibe shows that, for Chapelle, Racine had gone too far in reducing Bérénice's tragic stature.

understand the over-riding needs of the state (7, p.338). This is true while she doubts Titus's love for her; but, once he has convinced her of that love by the spectacle of his suffering, the innate virtue described at the beginning of Act II (ll.375-76) is at last able to make itself felt. The queen stands — which, in itself, symbolizes the return of her self-control and with it of her dignity. She finds herself able, for the first time, to appreciate the anguish of both of the men who love her (ll.1469-74), and, furthermore, to see that the empire is more important than she is. This is why she agrees to go in order to prevent Titus from putting his suicide threat into effect:

> Bérénice, Seigneur, ne vaut point tant d'alarmes,
> Ni que par votre amour l'univers malheureux,
> Dans le temps que Titus attire tous ses vœux
> Et que de vos vertus il goûte les prémices,
> Se voie en un moment enlever ses délices.
>
> (1484-88)

This monumental effort of self-control is impressive in itself, and all the more so since it follows so many scenes of bitter fury. More importantly still, Bérénice can be seen to be immediately and effortlessly overcoming the two tragic flaws which have exacerbated her predicament. First, there is her blindness. Although she showed early on that she was aware of the danger which Roman traditions might cause her (ll.639-41) and was explicitly reminded of it even earlier by Phénice (ll.292-96), she closed her mind to the threat. In so doing, she made her situation worse. Second, she had, up to and including the beginning of the play, been indulging in the same idyllic charade with virtue as Titus (see above, pp.70-71). Although she was sincere when she claimed to love Titus only for himself (ll.655-62), she loved him so much that she wanted him to be a good emperor so that the admiration of his subjects could amplify her love. This is why she was so carried away by the ceremonies which she describes at the end of Act I:

> Cette pourpre, cet or, que rehaussait sa gloire,

Et ses lauriers encor témoins de sa victoire;
Tous ces yeux qu'on voyait venir de toutes parts
Confondre sur lui seul leurs avides regards;
Ce port majestueux, cette douce présence.
Ciel! avec quel respect et quelle complaisance
Tous les cœurs en secret l'assuraient de leur foi!

(307-13)

It is only in Act V that she is finally able to recognize that, in a
Roman context, it is impossible for her to pursue Titus's love
and his virtue at the same time (cf. ll.161-62). As soon as she
does so, she is able to appreciate the sincerity of Titus's reasons
for sending her away, and, at the same time, the genuineness of
his love. This stills her deepest fears, leaving her free, for the
first time, to express her own love for him with moving
directness: 'J'aimais, Seigneur, j'aimais, je voulais être aimée'
(l.1479). The tragedy is that Titus and Bérénice must part
physically at the very moment when they are emotionally and
morally reconciled. Bérénice sublimates her love (ll.1491-92) in a
gesture of renunciation which enshrines it in a legendary tableau
where it will, by definition, have to remain unfulfilled:

Adieu. Servons tous trois d'exemple à l'univers
De l'amour la plus tendre et la plus malheureuse
Dont il puisse garder l'histoire douloureuse.

(1502-04)

These lines are sometimes interpreted as if Bérénice is
obtaining a devious self-satisfaction in making such a
monumental sacrifice (e.g. by J.D. Hubert, *17*, pp.129-30). This
is, however, wrong. If Bérénice can consign her love for Titus to
history, it is because the innermost fibres of her being are about
to be destroyed as she steps into the nightmare vision so
graphically evoked in Act IV. It is because she is facing this
terrifying prospect knowingly and deliberately and (unexpectedly for her) with no protestations or lamentations
whatsoever that she becomes truly majestic as she rises, speaks,
and quietly exits. She leaves the stage, indeed, with all the

majesty of a true queen, demonstrating as she does so that she was more than worthy to become the consort of the man on whose moral conversion she now sets the seal, but whose side she must leave for ever. This is why the end of the play creates the 'tristesse majestueuse' of which Racine rightly boasts in his preface.

Selective Bibliography

EDITIONS

1. The most convenient edition of the *Œuvres complètes* is in the Bibliothèque de la Pléiade series, edited by R. Picard, 2 vols (Paris: Gallimard, 1950-52). *Bérénice* is in vol. I, and is preceded by a short *Notice* in which Picard highlights the transformation in Titus's character when he becomes emperor.
2. *Bérénice*, edited by W.S. Maguiness (Manchester U.P., 1929). Has an annotated bibliography of seventeenth- and eighteenth-century criticism.
3. *Bérénice*, edited by C.L. Walton (Oxford U.P., 1965). Contains a useful introduction with a full survey of the arguments concerning the circumstances in which the two *Bérénice* plays were written.
4. *Bérénice*, edited by L. Lejealle (Paris: Nouveaux Classiques Larousse, 1971). The critical commentary sometimes needs to be read with care; but the *documentation thématique* and synopsis of critical judgments on the play are extremely useful. This is the edition to which I refer in the text.
5. Corneille's *Tite et Bérénice* is available in the "Intégrale" edition of the *Œuvres Complètes* by A. Stegman (Paris: Seuil, 1963).

GENERAL STUDIES OF RACINE

6. C. Abraham, *Jean Racine* (New York: Twayne, 1977).
7. A. Adam, *Histoire de la littérature française au XVIIe siècle,* vol. IV (Paris: Domat, 1954)
8. H.T. Barnwell, 'La gloire dans le théâtre de Racine', in *Jeunesse de Racine*, 1961 (pp.21-31), 1962 (pp.5-27), 1963 (pp.21-40), 1964 (pp.61-69), 1966 (pp.51-61), 1970-71 (pp.65-84).
9. ——, *The Tragic Drama of Corneille and Racine: an old parallel revisited* (Oxford: Clarendon Press, 1982). A brilliant reinterpretation of the relationship between Corneille and Racine in the light of the aesthetic principles and dramatic theories of the seventeenth century. Especially valuable for its reassessment of Racine's skills as a plot-maker.
10. R. Barthes, *Sur Racine* (Paris: Seuil, 1963). A challenging psychological analysis; but the discussion of *Bérénice* is based on the arbitrary assumption that Titus no longer loves the queen.
11. M. Descotes, *Les Grands Rôles du théâtre de Jean Racine* (Paris: P.U.F., 1957). Contains details of the performances of *Bérénice*, and a

rather cursory assessment of the difficulties involved in trying to act the part of the heroine.

12. N.K. Drown, *Jean Racine: meditations on his poetic art* (no place, 1982).

13. L. Dubech, *Jean Racine politique* (Paris: Grasset, 1926). Good analysis of the political factors, but makes insufficient allowance for the inwardly apprehended moral imperative experienced by Titus, and for the tragic flaws in the protagonists' make-up.

14. P. France, *Racine's Rhetoric* (Oxford: Clarendon Press, 1965). Essential reading. Contains a general survey of rhetoric in *Bérénice* (pp.185-95) and a short analysis of Titus's speech in V, 6 (pp.224-26). On the latter, see also *35*.

15. L. Goldmann, *Le Dieu caché* (Paris: Gallimard, 1959). A Marxist approach stressing the influence on Racine of the Jansenist vision of his educators.

16. W.D. Howarth, 'Some thoughts on the function of rhyme in French classical tragedy', in P.Bayley and D. Gabe Coleman (editors), *The Equilibrium of Wit: essays for Odette de Mourgues* (Lexington: French Forum, 1982), pp.150-56. Contains an interesting analysis of rhymes in *Bérénice* and *Tite et Bérénice*.

17. J.D. Hubert, *Essai d'exégèse racinienne* (Paris: Nizet, 1956). Excellent on Titus's self-destruction, but some of his deeper insights are not pushed to their natural conclusion.

18. R. Jasinski, *Vers le vrai Racine*, 2 vols (Paris: Colin, 1958). Exemplifies the biographical and historical approach, but takes his search for historical 'keys' to excessive extremes.

19. B. Knapp, *Jean Racine: mythos and renewal in modern theatre* (University of Alabama Press, 1971). Her use of myth as a tool of interpretation is rather extravagant, but worth reading.

20. R.C. Knight, 'The rejected source in Racine', in T.E. Lawrenson, F.E. Sutcliffe, G.F.A. Gadoffre (editors), *Modern Miscellany presented to Eugène Vinaver* (Manchester U.P., 1969), pp.154-66. A short but penetrating study suggesting a parallel between the ending of *Bérénice* and the 'conversion' scenes at the end of *Cinna* and *Nicomède*, but also emphasizing Racine's desire to demonstrate his originality by departing from his 'sources'.

21. J. Lapp. *Aspects of Racinian Tragedy* (University of Toronto Press, 1955). A brilliant analysis of the way in which Racine exploits seventeenth-century dramatic conventions.

22. C. Mauron, *L'Inconscient dans l'œuvre et la vie de Racine* (Paris: Corti, 1969). 'Psychocritical' study which tries to reveal Racine's 'obsessions affectives'. Sees Bérénice as both the mother figure from whom Titus wishes to escape and as one of the 'tendres amantes' he loves to torture. Rather extreme in his interpretations but makes some fascinating comparisons between *Bérénice*, *Andromaque* and *Britannicus*.

23. G. May, *Tragédie cornélienne, tragédie racinienne* (University of Illinois Press, 1948). Now somewhat dated, but still useful.
24. O. de Mourgues, *Racine or the Triumph of Relevance* (Cambridge U.P., 1967). One of the best general studies.
25. A. Niderst, *Les Tragédies de Racine: diversité et unité* (Paris: Nizet, 1975). Excellent interpretation of the dénouement of *Bérénice*.
26. V. Orgel, *A New View of the Plays of Racine* (London: Macmillan, 1948). Some insights into the character of Antiochus.
27. G. Pocock, *Corneille and Racine: problems of tragic form* (Cambridge U.P., 1973). Underestimates the dramatic potential of *Bérénice*, which he analyses as a 'poetic tragedy'. But he provides an excellent discussion of the themes of revelation and concealment and, in so doing, demonstrates the thematic importance of Antiochus.
28. J. Prophète, *Les Para-personnages dans les tragédies de Racine* (Paris: Nizet, 1981). Emphasizes the importance of Rome.
29. M. Turnell, *Jean Racine Dramatist* (London: Hamish Hamilton, 1972). Sometimes spurned by academic critics, but has some good insights into *Bérénice*.
30. C. Venesoen, *Jean Racine et le procès de la culpabilité* (Paris: Pensée Universelle, 1981). Stresses Titus's 'innocente culpabilité'.
31. E. Vinaver, *Racine et la poésie tragique* (Paris: Nizet, revised edition, 1963). Underestimates the importance of drama, but rightly regarded as one of the most stimulating books on Racine.
32. B. Weinberg, *The Art of Jean Racine* (University of Chicago Press, 1963). Has a good approach to Racine's dramatic technique, but tends to jump to rash conclusions about *Bérénice*.
33. P.J. Yarrow, *Racine* (Oxford: Blackwell, 1978). Contains a very useful chapter on style.

ON BERENICE

34. G. Antoine, *Racine: 'Bérénice'* (Paris: Centre de Documentation Universitaire, no date). Roneotyped Sorbonne lectures. Rather fussy presentation, but contains some penetrating stylistic analysis.
35. R.L. Barnett, 'Sur une scène de *Bérénice* (V, 6). Etude générative', *Lettres Romanes*, 31 (1977), pp.144-66. An analysis of Titus's ultimatum speech, endeavouring to support, through an analysis of style, Barthes's suggestion that Titus does not love Bérénice. Confuses the 'beau désordre' created by Racine with cool calculation on the part of the emperor.
36. P.F. Butler, 'La tragédie de *Bérénice*', *French Studies*, 3 (1949), pp.201-11. Sees Titus as consumed by a death-wish, and argues forcefully that the play is tragic.
37. W. Cloonan, 'Love and *gloire* in *Bérénice*: a Freudian perspective', *Kentucky Romance Quarterly*, 22 (1975), pp.517-25. Identifies Titus's *gloire* with Butler's death-wish.

38. J.A. Dainard, 'The power of the spoken word in *Bérénice*', *Romanic Review*, 67 (1976), pp.157-71. Overestimates the influence of the Roman senate, but a perceptive study of the problems of communication.

39. R. Emory, '*Bérénice* and the language of sight', *Romance Notes*, 19 (1978), pp.217-22. Applies Starobinski's approach.

40. L. Hermann, 'Vers une solution du problème des deux "Bérénices" ', *Mercure de France*, 15 avril 1928, pp.313-37. Argues, mainly on textual grounds, that Corneille stole his subject from Racine.

41. G. Michaut, *La 'Bérénice' de Racine* (Paris: Société française d'imprimerie et de librairie, 1907). Casts serious doubts on the tradition that Racine and Corneille were persuaded to write their Bérénice plays by Henriette d'Angleterre; but Michaut's own thesis (that Racine pirated Corneille's subject) is suspect because he is so anxious to prove that *Bérénice* is the most typical of Racine's plays. Contains valuable appendices, in which Michaut reprints Villars's *Critique de 'Bérénice'*.

42. R. McBride, 'Le rôle de Rome dans *Bérénice*', *Studi Francesi*, 18 (1974), pp.86-91. Short, but penetrating.

43. J. Morel, 'A propos de *Bérénice*: le thème du mariage des Romains et des reines dans la tragédie française du dix-septième siècle', in *Mélanges Pintard* (*Travaux de linguistique et de littérature* (Université de Strasbourg), XIII, 2 (1975)), pp.229-38. Very useful study showing that Racine's contemporaries would not necessarily have approved of the Roman anti-monarchical tradition.

44. F. Siguret, 'Bérénice/Impératrice: lecture d'une rime', *French Forum*, 3 (1978), pp.125-31.

45. E. Zimmermann, 'L'innocence et la tragédie chez Racine: le problème de *Bérénice*', *Papers on French Seventeenth-Century Literature*, 12 (Winter 1979-1980), pp.109-27. Reprinted as an appendix in the same author's *La Liberté et le destin dans le théâtre de Jean Racine* (Stanford: Anma Libri, 1982). Sees the fact that *Bérénice* does not conform with Racine's almost universal obsession with persecutors and innocent victims as proof that the subject of the play was suggested by Henriette d'Angleterre and subsequently pirated by Corneille. This interpretation makes no allowance for the fact that, whatever Racine's 'préoccupations obsessionnelles' may have been, his decision to write (or to agree to write) *Bérénice* will have been dictated by a conscious desire to follow *Britannicus* with a related but essentially very different play.

CRITICAL GUIDES TO FRENCH TEXTS

edited by
Roger Little, Wolfgang van Emden, David Williams